Research and Psychotherapy

Research and Psychotherapy

The Vital Link

Lester Luborsky and Ellen Luborsky

A JASON ARONSON BOOK
ROWMAN & LITTLEFIELD PUBLISHERS, INC.
Lanham • Boulder • New York • Toronto • Oxford

A JASON ARONSON BOOK

ROWMAN & LITTLEFIELD PUBLISHERS, INC.

Published in the United States of America
by Rowman & Littlefield Publishers, Inc.
A wholly owned subsidiary of The Rowman & Littlefield Publishing Group, Inc.
4501 Forbes Boulevard, Suite 200, Lanham, Maryland 20706
www.rowmanlittlefield.com

PO Box 317
Oxford
OX2 9RU, UK

British Library Cataloguing in Publication Information Available

Library of Congress Cataloging-in-Publication Data

Luborsky, Lester, 1920–
Research and psychotherapy : the vital link / Lester Luborsky and Ellen Luborsky.
p. cm.
"A Jason Aronson Book."
Includes bibliographical references and index.
ISBN-13: 978-0-7657-407-8 (cloth : alk. paper) ISBN: 978-0-7657-0407-8
ISBN-10: 0-7657-0407-2 (cloth : alk. paper)
ISBN-13: 978-0-7657-408-5 (pbk. : alk. paper)
ISBN-10: 0-7657-0408-0 (pbk. : alk. paper)
1. Supportive psychotherapy—Research. 2. Focused expressive psychotherapy—Research. 3. Psychoanalysis. I. Luborsky, Ellen. II. Title.
RC504.L835 2006
616.89'0072—dc22 2005023659

Printed in the United States of America

∞™ The paper used in this publication meets the minimum requirements of American National Standard for Information Sciences—Permanence of Paper for Printed Library Materials, ANSI/NISO Z39.48-1992.

Contents

Acknowledgments

Ellen and I, as coauthors of this book, wish to spread the knowledge on the vital link between research and psychotherapy. Other people have also applied their considerable editorial and psychological talents to make this book distinctive and generally better (e.g., Martin E. P. Seligman, George Vaillant, Jacques Barber, and Howard Book). Over many years, Martin E. P. Seligman's (Seligman & Csikszentmihalyi, 2000) emphasis on the relatively nonconflictual sources of personality has generated a new and growing field around that idea. George Vaillant (Vaillant, in press) has also inspired us with good models for this book. While the references will alert you to sources for the research and ideas presented here, the names used in the clinical examples are *all* fictitious.

The following friends and colleagues have all contributed their expertise to the making of this book. Most were psychotherapists whose clinical contribution to this book we very much wish to acknowledge. Many were psychiatric residents in our Department of Psychiatry who took part in individual or group supervision; some were staff or other colleagues. We profoundly thank each of them for their help in this monumentally huge task:

Jacques P. Barber, PhD
Ellen Berman, MD
Perry Berman, MD
Anna Rose Childress, PhD
Deborah Co, MD
Andrew Cooper, PhD
Paul Crits-Christoph, PhD
Jenna Ermold, BA
Thomas Gable, MD

Ruben Gur, PhD
Gagan Joshi, MD
Judith Kastenberg, MD
Bush Kavuru, MD
Susan Klebanoff, PhD
Beth Krause, PhD
Marc Lipschutz, MD
John Listerud, MD, PhD
George Luedke, MD
David Mark, PhD
Anita McLean, PhD
Fiona Mudge, MD
Sudha Nair, MD
John O'Reardon, MD
Maureen O'Reilly-Landry, PhD
Lorraine Pirro, MSW
David Roat, MD
Meyer Rothbart, MD
Moira Rynn, MD
Simrat Sethi, MD
Dipach Shah, MD
Stephen Stern, MD
Karen Stuart, PhD
Albert J. Stunkard, MD
Audrey Tyrka, MD, PhD
Carol Popp Weingarten, MD, PhD
Andrew Winokur, MD
Hao Xu, MD
Sharon Young, PhD

For the last three decades, for much of the support of my clinical and research studies, I gratefully acknowledge the United States Public Health Service (USPHS) Research Scientist Award 40710, and starting in 1968, I received yearly hard-money salary awards up through the year 2000.

Many professional organizations besides USPHS have encouraged me by their awards, including the American Psychological Association Clinical Division 12 Award (1986, 1995); the American Psychopathological Association's Paul H. Hoch Award (1996); the large and generous Sigourney Award Prize in Psychoanalysis (1997) (associated with the American Psychoanalytic Association through Bernard Pacella, a former president of the American Psychoanalytic Association); the American Psychological Association Gold Medal Award for Life Achievement (1999); the American Psychoanalytic Association Special Research Award (2000); and the Society for Psychotherapy Research special honorary award (2000) (arranged by Gregory Halperin).

All during this period, friends, colleagues, and relatives have had a helping relationship in this book's maturation. Outstanding among them were Howard Book for his popular guide, based on the first completely recorded SE treatment from beginning to end, titled *How to Practice Brief Psychodynamic Psychotherapy*. But it is Philip Holzman to whom thanks are given for his enthusiastic introduction of the idea of a *published* clinical guide, and to Martin E. P. Seligman, for his influential, extensive, and novel vistas through the backing of his "positive psychology."

Many other contributions, both papers and research studies, have included these names: Leslie Alexander, Marjorie Cohen, Arthur Auerbach, Gerald Aronson, George Woody, Frederic J. Levine, Stanley Greenspan, Ellen Berman, Perry Berman, Marshall Edelson, John Docherty, Paul Gerin, Jerome Frank (for his inspiring psychotherapy research and his writings on it), and Tomasz Andrusyna (for his skillful research assistant work within our group from 1999 to 2001).

All Luborskys were not only my indispensable relatives but also my good friends. They have each contributed in their own special ways: Ruth Samson Luborsky, PhD, was a brilliant writer in her own right in many fields, and art history was one of them; Ellen Luborsky, PhD, added her organizational, therapeutic, and editorial wisdom to her very special psychoanalytic writing talent; Lise Luborsky, Esq. added her fine legal skill; and Peter Luborsky, PhD, added his extraordinarily extensive multilanguage abilities. Miranda Outman-Kramer has aided us with her editorial talent and expertise, even suggesting the title of the book.

In the past decade, Lynne Siqueland of our Department of Psychiatry's Center for Psychotherapy Research (and now in private practice of SE psychotherapy) has supportive-expressively collaborated in enthusiastically coteaching with me my prizewinning annual psychotherapy seminar. She and Jacques Barber and some of the psychiatry residents helped with this new book; Jacques Barber's broad SE experience and sensitive presentational skill had a beneficial effect on this new manual and new book.

EARLY EXPERIENCES WITH INSPIRING COLLEAGUES

Large steps in my growth as a practitioner came during 5 successive years with each of five different Menninger Foundation colleagues as supervisors, each of whom themselves practiced both long-term psychotherapy and psychoanalysis: Lewis Robbins, Michalina Fabian, Irving Kartus, Albert Owers, and Carl Epstein. Naturally, therefore, I am highly appreciative of the system of yearly rotation of supervisors to help the early growth of younger colleagues, as well as of my lengthy opportunity to experience what personal psychoanalysis was like from the patient's viewpoint.

In addition, the input from each of three supervisors of my psychoanalytic training at the Topeka Psychoanalytic Institute is also reflected in my manual: Otto Fleishmann, Petrinella Tibout, and Ishak Ramzy. Otto Fleishmann, for example, lastingly impressed me with his precept: Have patience and listen to the patient, and wait until one has "the material" before drawing conclusions and deciding *what* to interpret and *how* to interpret it.

A few of my other great colleagues in those years who most influenced my theories of therapy and psychotherapeutic technique are Paul Bergman, Margaret Brenman, Rudolph Ekstein, Jan Frank, Merton Gill, Robert R. Holt, Philip Holzman, Helmut Kaiser, Walter Kass, Otto Kernberg, George Klein, Martin Mayman, Karl Menninger, Gardner Murphy, Lois Murphy, William Pious, David Rapaport, Benjamin Rubenstein, Roy Schafer, and Herbert Schlesinger. My style as a therapist became a personal admixture of what they offered.

CURRENT ASSISTANCE

This book could not have come to be without the patient assistance of Michael Crooks and Ramaris German, my research assistants at the University of Pennsylvania, and before them, Dan Kirk. They each have contributed valuable attention to the makings of this book.

Authors' Note

The clinical material in this book comes from two sources. Some of the cases were part of a research study in which the patients gave permission for the data to be used. In other cases, identifying information was deleted and composites were created in order to protect confidentiality.

Preface: The Book's Beginnings

Psychotherapy research has slowly but surely come into its own since my first book devoted to supportive-expressive (SE) psychotherapy was published in 1984. That book has been used around the world to train psychotherapists and as a manual that has furthered research on SE psychotherapy.

An impressive example of the growth of SE research emerged from the Department of Psychotherapy and Psychosomatic Medicine, University of Ulm, Germany, sparked by Horst Kächele's leadership (and before him by Helmut Thomae's). This research-oriented clinical center has a huge research staff and offers wonderful worldwide clinical and research conferences employing SE psychotherapy concepts such as the Core Conflictual Relationship Theme (CCRT) conferences in December 1981, December 1982, September 2000, and January 2003.

Some of the readers of my 1984 book helped guide translations into other languages, including German (Luborsky, 1998, translated by Hans-Joachim Grünzig), Italian (Luborsky, 1989, translated by Paola Azzone and Raffaella Ferrari, with the administrative help of Salvatore Freni), Portuguese (Luborsky, 1998, by Henrique Kiperman), Japanese (Luborsky, 1990, by Yasuhiko Taketomo), French (Luborsky, 1996, by Josée Gaudet, with Louis Diguer as consultant), and Russian (Luborsky, 2003, by Katherine Kalmykova).

While clinical research findings on SE psychotherapy have grown during the last 20 years, they have not been integrated into knowledge about clinical practice. In addition, the high profile given to the use of medication to treat psychological conditions has tended to obscure the attention paid to clinical and research methods. These are among the current conditions that prompted this book. Our goal is to explain the clinical principles of supportive-expressive (SE) psychotherapy, to update the mushrooming of research advances made by the new techniques, and to explore the link between the two.

RECOGNIZING THE LINK

For many years, the attention given to the advances of psychotherapy research was far less than had been hoped for, in spite of decades of psychotherapy research (Luborsky & McLellan, 1981; McLellan, Luborsky, Woody, O'Brien, & Druley, 1983). I even dared to publish an article on this theme as early as 1969, titled "Research Cannot Yet Influence Clinical Practice." My views then paralleled those of Carl Rogers, and I was even given a joint prize with him. His work was based on his own psychotherapy research, which was prodigious in productivity, diversity, and innovation. Yet according to Rogers, his views had little effect on the form and even on the content of his influential clinical practice at the time (personal communication, about 1960).

Since then I've radically changed my views. In the last two decades, psychotherapy research has actually accelerated its impact on clinical practice. Two important examples validate the link between the principles of dynamic psychotherapy and clinical research: (1) the consistently positive predictive value of the Helping Alliance (Luborsky, 1976; Morgan, Luborsky, Crits-Christoph, Curtis, & Solomon, 1982; Luborsky, Crits-Christoph, Alexander, Margolis, & Cohen, 1983; Luborsky, 1994) and (2) the guidance for interpreting the transference patterns offered by the Core Conflictual Relationship Theme (CCRT) method (Luborsky, 1977; Luborsky & Crits-Christoph, 1998).

MY BACKGROUND

I have searched for decades for methods of studying psychotherapy, some of which are highlighted in this book. The background for that quest began with an immersion in psychodynamic methods at the Menninger Foundation, where both classical psychoanalysis and dynamic psychotherapy were practiced. During my training and work at the Menninger Foundation (1947 to 1959), the development of psychotherapy research was also considered important. During the last 6 years, I participated in the Menninger Foundation Psychotherapy Research Project. The commingling of learning to do treatment with doing research was formative in my quest.

However, an earlier event actually prompted my career direction. In 1938, while studying at Penn State University, I stumbled upon Freud's collected papers in my landlady's library. I had at first majored in botany, as I had long intended. But after reading this book, I decided to give up my old intention to major in botany and changed to a major in psychology.

From Menninger, I moved to the University of Pennsylvania in 1959 to start the Penn Psychotherapy Project, which was pivotal in the development of the CCRT. While working at the University of Pennsylvania, my supervision of psychiatrists, psychologists, and social workers furthered my thinking about the clinical principles and methods in supportive-expressive psychotherapy. These experiences also helped me develop the theory of SE psychotherapy, as described in this book.

A big push came from the supervisees' appreciation of my very first book on psychotherapy, *The Task of the Psychotherapist* (1973). My intention to write about SE psychotherapy was heartened as well by the way the psychiatric residents in our Department of Psychiatry reciprocated my appreciation of them by voting me the recipient of Penn Departmental Awards for teaching on three formal occasions: the 1977 Earl Bond Award for Excellence in Teaching in the Department of Psychiatry, the 1980 residency class award for outstanding contribution to psychiatric education, and the 1997 Excellence in Teaching Award of the Department of Psychiatry, University of Pennsylvania, "for contribution to residency education by Lester Luborsky and Lynne Siqueland" (my coteacher for several years).

THE BOOK'S SECTIONS

Research and Psychotherapy: The Vital Link has five main sections: Section 1 offers an exposition of the nature of SE psychotherapy's techniques and their relation to research. Section 2 describes clinical research methods that are relevant to the study of dynamic treatment. Section 3 gives an account of SE psychotherapy via a manual format, including an exposition of its principles, along with clinical examples. The tasks that form the body of the manual, covered in chapters 8 through 12, include the following topics: the opening phase of treatment (chapter 8), the supportive techniques (chapter 9), the expressive techniques for understanding (chapter 10), the expressive techniques for responding (chapter 11), and the closing phase of SE psychotherapy (chapter 12). Section 4 reviews forms of psychotherapy and combinations of treatments, while section 5 summarizes the issues in the vital link between research and psychotherapy.

PART I

THE VITAL LINK BETWEEN RESEARCH AND PSYCHOTHERAPY

Chapter One

The Links between Research and Psychotherapy

Psychotherapy and research are typically different domains, without much exchange between the two. Among the challenges of bringing them together is that researchers and clinicians use different methods of inquiry and are often suspicious of the procedures of the other. Those who practice psychotherapy may be wary of research, due to concerns that it might reduce or distort clinical findings. Researchers may be dubious about the value of clinical discoveries since they are not found through a scientific method. But there are ways to bring these domains together that do not violate the essence of either one. How is that possible? That is the topic of this book.

If the research methods used to examine psychotherapy do not fit with the nature of the process, the research does run the risk of missing important elements. By developing research methods that can measure the forms of discovery that take place in clinical practice, we can link research and psychotherapy in a meaningful way. The clinical research methods described in this book do just that (see the chapters on the CCRT and on the Symptom-Context method). They grow out of a clinical understanding and are then applied in ways that meet scientific standards for validity.

For clinical research to be valid, researchers need to be examining the same process. Two treatments can have the same name but actually be conducted very differently. Researchers solve this problem in different ways, often by looking for treatments with clear guidelines. In this book, we offer guidelines for supportive-expressive (SE) psychotherapy to ensure that clinicians and researchers are on the same topic when exploring its efficacy.

SE psychotherapy is an operational version of dynamic psychotherapy, one that is both widely practiced and well studied, making it an ideal template to examine how clinical research and clinical practice can come together. To do that, this book will explain the principles and methods of SE psychotherapy. It will also explain research methods that lend themselves both to the study of psychotherapy and to its practice.

Research and Psychotherapy: The Vital Link is written for psychotherapists who want to find ways to add a more scientific dimension to their work. It is equally written for researchers who wish to understand how to keep their research relevant to clinical practice. Both groups may expand the potential of their work by examining the principles and guidelines presented here.

EVIDENCE-BASED PRACTICE

In order to address the question of which treatments have empirical validation, a movement toward evidence-based practice has emerged. Evidence-based practice gives credence to forms of treatment supported by certain kinds of research evidence, notably randomly controlled studies. The American Psychological Association has begun an initiative to develop empirically supported therapies (Task Force on Psychological Intervention Guidelines, 1995).

On the surface, this idea sounds like a good one. Finding empirical support for forms of treatment could guide therapists toward effective results and guide patients toward appropriate choices in treatment. However, the way that idea has been carried out so far does not necessarily lead to better treatment. In order to have a "clean" study, researchers select patients and methods that fit with their research design. This approach leaves out the complexity of the personality and dynamics of the patient (Westen, Novotny, & Thompson-Brenner, 2004).

It also neglects the question of the allegiance of the researcher, which has been found to be a significant factor influencing outcome in studies comparing forms of psychotherapy (Luborsky, Rosenthal, et al., 2002). The differences among the target concepts in the treatments can affect comparisons. If the treatments have similar, or *convergent*, concepts, the variables that are studied have a high degree of agreement; when they are *contentious*, they do not. Larger allegiance differences are found when studying contentious treatments, notably those contrasting behavioral and dynamic therapies (Luborsky & Barrett, in press). This means that the comparisons may sound more objective than they actually are.

Evidence-based practice brings with it the assumption that *DSM-IV* disorders are themselves what psychotherapy should treat, although as Westen et al. (2004) point out, those categories were created by committee rather than by empirical research. Therapies with specific methods for addressing the symptoms of Axis I disorders, such as cognitive-behavioral therapy, are most often cited as meeting those criteria.

However, dynamic psychotherapy has important—but still relatively neglected—research evidence to support it as well. In reviewing that evidence, an alternate approach to the meanings and treatment of symptoms will also emerge. The findings about SE psychotherapy are presented here, as are central factors for effective psychotherapy, regardless of the therapist's orientation.

ORIENTATIONS IN PSYCHOTHERAPY

While the research movement of evidence-based practice continues to look for the most effective form of psychotherapy for specific disorders, the trend in the practice of psychotherapy has been toward *eclectic combinations of treatments*. That trend is found not only among the psychologists who do psychotherapy but also in the helping professions generally. Some examples from among practicing psychologists follow: Of 546 psychotherapists in the Clinical Division of the American Psychological Association (APA) who returned the questionnaire, 27% were eclectic, 24% were cognitive, and 18% were psychodynamic (Norcross, Karg, & Prochaska, 1997). In the Division of Psychotherapy of the APA, this trend has also been found to be similar for 477 practitioners—30% eclectic, 28% psychodynamic, and 28% cognitive (Norcross, Prochaska, & Farber, 1993). Of 538 psychologists in the APA Division of Psychotherapy, the results were 30% eclectic, with 21% psychodynamic and 16% cognitive (Norcross, Hedges, & Castle, 2001). The results typically begin with analytic methods and go on to psychodynamic and cognitive methods in that order. Although psychiatrists and psychologists had similar percentages until recently, the results are now ambiguous since many psychiatrists have shifted their time toward doing psychopharmacological treatment instead.

Dynamic psychotherapy is nevertheless one of the most common of the major psychotherapies in the United States, Europe, Australia, and many other parts of the world. SE psychotherapy is a well-defined form of dynamic psychotherapy (Eagle, Wolitzky, & Luborsky, 2001) that continues to be practiced in both outpatient mental health clinics and in private practice.

EFFECTIVE PSYCHOTHERAPY

Which form of psychotherapy is the most effective? That has been the topic of many research studies, including large-scale meta-analyses. Although these studies have never proven one form of psychotherapy to be consistently better than all the others, they indicate that psychotherapies tend toward beneficial outcomes (Luborsky, Singer, & Luborsky, 1975; Smith, Glass, & Miller,

1980; Lambert, Shapiro, & Bergin, 1986; Rosenthal, 1990). This research result, sometimes called the "equivalence effect," has come to be known as "the Dodo bird finding" after the story of the Dodo bird in Lewis Carroll's *Alice in Wonderland*, which was linked with this finding when it first emerged (Luborsky, Singer, & Luborsky, 1975). In that story, the Dodo bird serves as the judge for a race and proclaims, "Everyone has won, and all must have prizes."

The same conclusion applies to forms of psychotherapy, where all win the race for benefits. Patients achieve "some" to "much" benefit in psychotherapy; the research implies that psychotherapy works. The Dodo bird's prizes are not only for the qualities within each type of psychotherapy but also for the fundamental factors common to well-practiced psychotherapies, sometimes referred to as "g" (general) factors.

In conclusion, several large-scale studies have repeatedly found that while psychotherapy itself has benefits, there tend to be only nonsignificant differences among the outcomes of the different forms of psychotherapy (Luborsky, Rosenthal, et al., 2002). In research terms, this finding is one of nonsignificant differences.

WHY HIGHLIGHT SE PSYCHOTHERAPY?

SE dynamic psychotherapy has been shown to be as successful as any of the best-performing psychotherapies it has been compared with (Luborsky, Rosenthal, et al., 2002). The evidence over the years confirms that this form of psychotherapy, like the best of psychotherapies (Lambert & Bergin, 1994), *helps at least moderately about two thirds to three quarters of the patients.*

The importance that SE psychotherapy gives to the alliance between therapist and patient has been amply supported by research. The strength of the Helping Alliance turns out to be a major predictor of outcome (Luborsky, 1976; Morgan, Luborsky, Crits-Christoph, Curtis, & Solomon, 1982; Luborsky, Crits-Christoph, Alexander, Margolis, & Cohen, 1983; Miller, Luborsky, Barber, & Docherty, 1993; Luborsky, 1994). While all forms of treatment require some degree of alliance to function, dynamic psychotherapy is unique in the explicit focus on its development.

SE psychotherapy is suited to a wide range of patients, through a planned mix of supportive and expressive techniques. This allows it to be adapted to patients with different needs and degrees of pathology. That flexibility also makes it useful for patients with a combination of symptoms, whose problems cannot be neatly defined by one *DSM-IV* category. The potential, through expressive work, to understand present and past relationship problems offers a clinical method for shifting long-standing, maladaptive patterns. Changes in the Core Conflictual Relationship Theme (CCRT) reflect the process of change that can occur in dynamic psychotherapy, one that can be measured in psychotherapy research (Luborsky & Crits-Christoph, 1998).

A CONSISTENT APPROACH TO PREDICTION OF OUTCOME

My 1984 book, *Principles of Psychoanalytic Psychotherapy*, served as a psychotherapy manual, in order to bring consistency to practice and a standard to research. When doing clinical research, it is necessary that the psychotherapy be consistent in its methods, otherwise the study may not actually be examining the same form of treatment. Using a manual helps ensure the validity of the study. The SE section of this present book can serve that function, since it fits the definition of a psychotherapy manual (Luborsky & DeRubeis, 1984, as detailed later in this section). While manuals for treatments for specific symptoms have sprung up in recent years, this book, along with the 1984 manual, is among the few full-scale guides to any of the forms of psychotherapy that can be used with diverse problems and symptoms, including "comorbid," or interwoven, problems.

This book began as a Socratic dialogue, but it now offers an integrated set of principles and methods on how to practice SE psychotherapy, allowing therapists to be grounded in the essentials of the treatment. Therapists may fear that such a guide could cramp their clinical freedom. However, these principles actually encourage a therapist's freedom to make clinically meaningful decisions.

Three essential aspects of this guide to SE allow it to function as a manual for those who will be using it as a basis for research.

The *first* component of a psychotherapy manual is that it contains an exposition of the main principles of psychotherapy. It explains the principles of SE psychotherapy, which are originally based on Freud's recommendations for psychoanalytic techniques (1911/1958, 1912a/1958, 1912b/1958, 1913a/1958, 1913b/1958, 1914/1958, 1915a/1957, 1915b/1958, 1926/1959, 1932/1964, 1937/1964). Some were added or refined at the Menninger Foundation over the six or seven decades of this SE manual's course of development.

The *second* part of the manual points out the distinctive essence of SE psychotherapy. It is a concrete guide for therapists on how to practice SE techniques. This treatment manual makes clear those techniques and makes each technique more vivid through clinical examples.

The *third* part of the manual consists of scales to measure the degree to which the therapist actually does the recommended techniques of SE psychotherapy, an essential for research studies, so that there is a degree of certainty about what is being studied. Such scales used to be routinely missing but now have become routinely present, as noted in *Encyclopedia of Psychotherapy* (Luborsky, 2002). The degree to which the therapist has carried out the manual's principles can be seen when independent judges apply manual-based rating forms to samples of the therapist's sessions. These forms are based on Luborsky, Woody, McLellan, O'Brien, and Rosenzweig (1982), with alternate forms by Barber and Crits-Christoph (1996) and Barber, Krakauer, Calvo, Badgio, and Faude (1997).

THE BOOK'S INNOVATIONS

It covers the new research studies on the clinical techniques. This book is rare in its coverage of the empirical research on treatment techniques, especially compared with other manuals in our field. Since the book clarifies SE dynamic concepts, it is unique in applying empirical methods to clinical phenomena in the same volume. That is intended as an impetus to the process of turning up research ideas and methods in psychotherapy, and in dynamic psychotherapy in particular.

Its format is well suited for training. This book can serve as a guide in the training of beginning therapists, as well as a resource for experienced therapists who wish to further improve their skills. It is also a useful companion to consult during *supervision*. The scales for measuring the treatment techniques can be used to determine the degree to which a therapist has mastered SE psychotherapy and is following the recommendations of the manual. For *teachers*, the book provides an integrated and reformed introduction to clinical practice and research. It also makes an ideal starting point for *students* who are writing dissertations.

It clarifies the therapist's understanding. Throughout the long history of SE psychotherapy, the specifics of the process by which the therapist draws inferences from the patient's communications have been largely neglected (Ramzy, 1974; Ramzy & Shevrin, 1976). An aim of this manual is to help the therapist's task of understanding the patient's motives—her intentionality through her point of view (as discussed by George Klein, 1970).

A helpful scheme for formulating the therapist's understanding is provided by the CCRT method (see chapter 4 for further explanations of CCRT). This method specifies the CCRT principles for understanding the three-part relationship theme: the patient's main wishes; the expressed responses from others, including the therapist; and the responses of the self. The content of this theme in terms of the CCRT can then serve as a guide for tracing the therapist's interpretative responses to the patient.

It is a guide to fostering the supportive relationship with the patient. This book offers a guide to how to best foster a supportive relationship (chapter 9). While the role of support in treatment is often minimized or considered unimportant, research has shown a consistent positive correlation between the patient's experience of feeling supported and the outcomes of treatment. The chapter on supportive relationships explores the experience of support and the ways it can be enhanced in treatment, especially through the Helping Alliance.

It provides an alternative to guides on empirically supported psychotherapies. This book illustrates how research can emerge from clinical process rather than be imposed on it. Unlike current research studies on empirically supported psychotherapy, which typically test a specific treatment for a disorder defined by *DSM-IV*, the approach to clinical research highlighted here parallels the ways that therapists make clinical discoveries. The book offers the potential to study processes that have their origins in the principles and observations of psychotherapists.

NEW METHODS AND FINDINGS

Here are some of the new clinical approaches and research studies that are relevant to making links between research and psychotherapy.

1. New Clinical Research Findings

There are now many more comparative studies of different psychotherapies (Lambert & Bergin, 1994). Nonsignificant difference is the most common result in these studies, but more is now known about this nonsignificant difference result in comparisons of treatments (Luborsky, Rosenthal, et al., 2002).

We now know more about the role of the researcher's allegiance to the form of psychotherapy being studied. It turns out to be a major factor in restudies of outcomes of comparisons of treatments (Luborsky, Rosenthal, et al., 2002; Luborsky, Barrett, et al., in preparation).

But exceptions have been found to that trend; the researchers' allegiance is not always a major factor in outcome. A prime example is that of the National Institute for Drug Abuse Study of Cocaine Abuse (Crits-Christoph, Siqueland, et al., 1998), a four-site study of cocaine abuse. In that study, researchers' alliances did not apparently play a major part—most of the researchers had an allegiance toward psychotherapy, but in fact, drug counseling itself was found to be the most effective treatment.

2. New CCRT Studies

Recent studies of the CCRT break new ground. There is now evidence of its neurologic underpinnings (Loughead et al., in preparation), of its existence apart from treatment (Barber, Luborsky, Crits-Chistoph, & Diguer, 1995), and of the nature of its changes during treatment (Luborsky & Crits-Christoph, 1998) (see chapter 4).

3. New Uses of the Symptom-Context Method

The Symptom-Context method began as a research method that follows clinical observations on the meanings of symptoms. However, it can be used in psychotherapy as well, to decode symptoms through their links to the immediate context. It can be particularly useful in the treatment of anxiety and post-traumatic stress disorder (see chapter 5).

This method has considerable potential for both studying and treating stress-related medical problems. This is illustrated through its use in understanding the context for recurrent headaches. It is further demonstrated through the parallel research of Carels et al. (2003), who found a positive correlation between negative emotion and arrhythmias of the heart.

4. Bringing Viewpoints Together

During the time interval since 1984, there has been a surge in biological explanations for what were once considered psychological problems. While this has brought vital new knowledge into the field, some have seen it as replacing psychological inquiry. An aim of this book is to fight against such splits into oppositional models and instead to support a more rounded and integrated proficiency in psychotherapy. Developing psychiatrists, psychologists, neurologists, counselors, and social workers all need to learn from each other rather than be presented one side of a complex whole.

Validation for this integrated view comes through current research on the neurologic underpinnings of the CCRT (mentioned previously). Through such studies, we can see both the neurological and psychological view of what is actually the same event.

Chapter Two

The Essence of Supportive-Expressive (SE) Psychotherapy

Supportive-expressive (SE) psychotherapy is in itself an essence—an essence of dynamic psychotherapy, made operational and "user friendly" through techniques that can be used in practice and in research. It can be traced back to psychoanalysis, which is the grand old treatment in terms of its age and intensiveness (Luborsky, 2000b). Ever since Freud (1911/1958, 1912a/1958, 1912b/1958, 1913a/1958, 1914/1958, 1915b/1958) first spelled out his treatment recommendations in his pioneer techniques papers, these techniques have influenced both psychoanalysis and the dynamic psychotherapies that followed from it. Among the basic sources for the treatment explications are Fenichel (1938), Stone (1951), Menninger and Holzman (1973), Wallerstein (1986), and Luborsky (2000b).

SE psychotherapy takes its essence from the principles of dynamic psychotherapy and integrates them with innovative research methods that were derived from clinical-quantitative observations, such as in the Core Conflictual Relationship Theme (CCRT) method (Luborsky, 1977; Luborsky & Crits-Christoph, 1990, 1998), the Helping Alliance method (Luborsky, 1976, 2000), and the Symptom-Context method (Luborsky, 1996).

That makes this SE version of dynamic psychotherapy distinctive because (1) it gives the therapist tools to guide the treatment; (2) it gives a system to conceptualize and to score processes that are often difficult to capture, such as the sources of symptoms or of a persisting pattern in relationships; and (3) it provides the researcher with tools to further explore change processes in psychotherapy.

THE BACKGROUND OF SE DYNAMIC PSYCHOTHERAPY

In the century-long period since Freud launched his descriptions of treatment techniques, dynamic psychotherapy has become differentiated from psychoanalysis, although this offspring retains many resemblances to that of its parent.

The first distinctions were made by Ferenczi (1950) and Rank (1936) in order to satisfy the needs of patients and therapists *to shorten psychoanalysis*. Alexander and French (1946) continued their drive toward shortening such treatments, with the aim of making a treatment like psychoanalysis more affordable. Length and intensity of treatment have also been modified to accommodate the needs and lives of patients.

Some newer treatments were shortened to within the length of brief psychotherapy. According to Butcher and Koss (1978), "Today . . . 25 sessions is the upper-limit of 'brief' therapy" (p. 730). Also as the basis for crisis interventions during the Second World War, Grinker and Spiegel (1944, 1945) and Lindemann (1944) worked out a brief treatment of only one to three sessions. These treatment methods are very, very short term. They can be applied where immediate intervention is required and little time is available.

The second motive for change *was a need for a psychotherapy that could be adapted to a wider range of patients*, including those with poor psychological health who are frequently unable to cope with the intensity of psychoanalysis. SE is intended as a flexible treatment, with depth and duration of the treatment tailored to suit the needs of each patient.

In order to *cull the treatment for its essential principles*, we have purposely slighted metapsychological studies in favor of the more clinical ones, so these papers are mostly free of unessential metapsychological language. The principles were derived from commonalties across this sample of papers: Bergmann and Hartman (1977); Bibring (1954); Freud (1911/1958, 1912a/1958, 1912b/1958, 1913a/1958, 1914/1958, 1915b/1958); Gill (1951, 1954); Greenson (1967); Hollender (1965); Luborsky, Fabian, Hall, Ticho, and Ticho (1958); Schlesinger (1969); Stone (1961); Wallerstein, Robbins, Sargent, and Luborsky (1956); and Wallerstein (1986).

SE psychotherapy has gone through a very long period of maturation. Since about 1940, a lot of the standard treatments at the Menninger Foundation have been called either "supportive-expressive" or "expressive-supportive," depending on which of its two main techniques predominated. While the version presented here grows out of that tradition, it is now referred to simply as "SE" and is distinctive for its clinical specifics and its research methods.

PRINCIPLES BEHIND SE PSYCHOTHERAPY

The methods used in SE psychotherapy are linked to the basic principles of dynamic psychotherapy, which have evolved from some of the cornerstone concepts of psychoanalysis. That process of transformation is summarized in table 2.1. The central principles follow:

1. The transference, Freud's discovery of a "template" for repetitions of patterns in relationships, remains central to the theory and technique in dynamic treatment. In SE psychotherapy, the CCRT gives a way to delineate relationship patterns. Both the concept and the method will be explained further in chapter 4.
2. A positive therapeutic relationship forms a base for dynamic psychotherapy, reminiscent of Freud's original recommendation to "let be" a positive transference. In SE psychotherapy, the Helping Alliance methods provide ways to enhance the positive experience of the therapeutic relationship.
3. The third crucial principle is that of unconscious motives and conflict. Conflict between parts of the self that are outside of full awareness can take the form of symptoms or "acting out." In dynamic treatment, as in psychoanalysis, efforts are made to "make the unconscious conscious" in order to help bring warded-off parts of the self into awareness. In SE psychotherapy, the Symptom-Context method gives a symptom-focused structure to the inquiry (see chapter 5).

Table 2.1. Principles behind SE Psychotherapy

PSYCHOANALYTIC THEORY	*DYNAMIC PSYCHOTHERAPY*	*SE PSYCHOTHERAPY*	*RESEARCH POSSIBILITIES*
1. Transference	Work through the transference in treatment	CCRT methods	Use CCRT to study the process of psychotherapy
2. A positive therapeutic relationship is a good base for treatment	Attend to the therapeutic relationship	Helping Alliance methods	Examine role of Helping Alliance in medical and psychological cure
3. Unconscious conflict can result in symptoms	Explore sources and manifestations of conflict	Symptom-Context method	Use the Symptom-Context method to study symptom formation

CHANGE IN SE PSYCHOTHERAPY

At the core of dynamic treatment are two central elements that combine to create the conditions for change (see table 2.2). The first is an exploration of the nature and sources of the problems that have led the patient into treatment. Inner conflict that has been made manifest through symptoms becomes instead a topic in treatment. A process of self-understanding unfolds through the use of expressive techniques, made clear through the Core Conflictual Relationship Theme method and the Symptom-Context method.

The second element that creates the potential for change comes through the nature and structure of the therapeutic relationship. Supportive techniques bring the patient a sense of being helped, which is less about the content of the work than about the experience of the Helping Alliance.

CHANGE IN PSYCHOANALYTIC THEORY

The potential for change through analytic work comes from its ability to restructure the elements of a patient's "psychic life." By setting up a process that is home to all thoughts and feelings the patient may have, *the treatment includes both the known and the previously unknown parts of the self.* Dreams, daydreams, memories, and random thoughts are all invited into the process so that a fuller version of the self may begin to be understood.

In that process, patterns and problems in relationships with others take a forefront position. The relationship with the analyst provides a key to the examination of relationship problems. The transference of old patterns and expectations to the analyst is noted as it emerges so that the patient and analyst can clear a path for new ways of being. SE psychotherapy holds true to the fundamental analytic concepts but uses new methods to keep them in the forefront of the treatment. Those methods bring clarity to a sometimes mysterious process.

THEORY MEETS RESEARCH

How much does clinical research support these theories and practices? Is there any empirical support for these views of therapeutic change? While psychoanalytic theory has been tested and transformed through clinical practice over the past century, there is now research that supports the basic principles and methods just described.

A positive Helping Alliance turns up repeatedly as linked with good treatment outcome (Horvath, Gaston, & Luborsky, 1993). That is true when con-

Table 2.2. Change in SE Psychotherapy

Change	*Patient*	*Therapist*
1. Understanding the specific CCRT pattern	1. Through increasing awareness of the CCRT in his relationships	1. By helping the patient notice the CCRT in the different facets of his life
2. Understanding the connection between the CCRT and the patient's symptoms	2. Through growing awareness of links between symptoms and CCRT	2. By helping the patient notice the links
3. Changes in symptoms and shifts in the negative components of the CCRT	3. Through mastery over 1 and 2; helps change old patterns of expression	3. By helping the patient work through the CCRT as it emerges in sessions and in life
4. The Helping Alliance expands	4. By experiencing an ally in the therapist and in the therapy	4. By facilitating the growth of the Helping Alliance
5. The gains of the treatment are increasingly under the patient's control	5. By internalizing the work of the treatment	5. By encouraging the patient's efforts at mastery
6. Patient feels ready to handle her own life	6. By consolidating the understandings gained in treatment	6. By helping the patient with the personal meanings of the treatment and the termination

sidered from the perspective of the patient, the therapist, and the independent raters (Luborsky, Crits-Christoph, Mintz, and Auerbach, 1988). Those results bolster the importance given to the alliance in SE.

What about the exploratory work, which is what distinguishes dynamic treatment from other commonly practiced psychotherapies? That has proven more difficult to measure, since it involves an internal process of change. However, the CCRT gives a way to look into that process. It turns out that patients with a good treatment outcome have often gone through a transformation in the patterns of their CCRTs. Their wishes remain their wishes, essentially unchanged from the time they started treatment. But the typically negative responses they expect from others or the self-defeating responses from the self are no longer so typical. This gives the patient greater freedom to try new ways to actualize their wishes (Levine & Luborsky, 1981).

What about the premise that aspects of the patient's struggle could be unconscious? Is there research support for such a notion? After decades of skepticism over the existence of an unconscious mind, support now comes from clinical and clinical-quantitative research (Shevrin, Bond, Brakel, Hertel, & Williams, 1996.) as well as from neuroscience (Aine, 1995). How states of consciousness may shift during treatment remains a topic for further study.

NINE ESSENTIAL PRINCIPLES OF SE PSYCHOTHERAPY: A SUMMARY

Principle 1: Develop a Positive Helping Alliance

Developing a positive Helping Alliance is a crucial aspect of SE psychotherapy. While most patients experience it more as the therapist giving them help (Helping Alliance, type 1), and some experience it more as a partnership between the patient and therapist (Helping Alliance, type 2), both forms help bring a relational structure and a sense of support to the therapy. A positive Helping Alliance has been consistently linked with a later successful treatment outcome (Luborsky, Crits-Christoph, et al., 1988).

Principle 2: Evaluate the Psychological Health of the Patient

In order to guide the treatment, it is helpful to have a sense of the severity of the patient's problems. The level of overall initial Health-Sickness tends to correlate with the outcome of treatment (Luborsky, Crits-Christoph, et al., 1988). In other words, for better and for worse, health generates health, and severity of the illness makes for a more difficult recovery. This is most particularly true in the presence of psychosis.

However, the Health-Sickness level can help the therapist make an optimal plan by giving more support to patients at lower levels of functioning and by enhancing the expressive focus for others. It helps guide decisions about the structure and emphasis of the treatment.

Principle 3: Establish the Structure of the Treatment

In the beginning of the treatment, the therapist and the patient should decide on the appropriate treatment structure. That includes both the question of the frequency of the sessions and the question as to whether it will be a *time-limited* or an *open-ended* treatment. These decisions are based on clinical and on clinical-practical factors.

SE time-limited, or *session-limited*, is a short-term treatment that tends to run from about 8 to 25 sessions. It is defined by its time limit and is most useful either for patients who have one focal issue to solve or for those who cannot engage in a longer treatment for practical reasons. In *open-ended SE*, the patient and therapist settle on the length of treatment as it unfolds, based on the nature of the problems and the progress of the work. SE tends to be a treatment of moderate length, ranging from a few months to several years—as long as is needed to achieve the goals.

The most common frequency for SE psychotherapy is once or twice per week, with once being most common. Once-weekly sessions give a reliable structure to the week and the work. Sessions are held twice a week for two opposite reasons. The first is to intensify the expressive work for patients who will benefit from more depth of exploration in order to uncover the sources of their problems. The second is to amplify the support given by the treatment for patients who are having difficulty functioning in daily life.

Principle 4: Use Supportive Techniques

Supportive techniques (see chapter 9) are noncognitive in the sense that they are not really aimed at providing understanding, although they can set the stage for it. Instead, they are aimed at creating a safe setting and safe relationship to allow the therapy to unfold.

An essential aspect of the supportive conditions comes from the treatment structure itself. That includes the consistency of regular appointments as well as the sense that the therapist and patient are working together to achieve the patient's goals.

Another aspect of support comes from the nonjudgmental, accepting stance of the therapist. The therapist's empathy for the patient's emotional experience, and the therapist's ability to listen to the patient, can make a profound difference in the "feel" of the therapy. A third form of support is a discussion of the practical aspects of the patient's life, including encouragement, through coping with the problems of daily living. This form is particularly relevant for patients who have trouble holding onto an adequate level of functioning.

Principle 5: Use Expressive Techniques

The expressive techniques (see chapters 10 and 11) are central to what differentiates dynamic psychotherapy from other common treatments. Ample expressive work turns psychotherapy into a process of self-discovery. When the patient has the freedom to speak unspoken thoughts, it can awaken his curiosity and his awareness.

These techniques encourage the patient to express thoughts and feelings, allowing the therapist and patient to reflect on them and explore their meanings. One of the most potent revelations comes from the reexperiencing of the early relationship problems that have become part of the current relationship patterns.

Principle 6: Use the CCRT Method as a Guide to Understanding and Fashioning Interventions

The CCRT brings the complex process of discerning relationship patterns into view so that the CCRT can focus the interventions. It is a prime tool to test hypotheses in psychotherapy research because it offers a way to code clinical concepts that were previously gained through intuition alone.

The CCRT is central in supportive-expressive psychotherapy for these reasons: (1) the CCRT provides an understanding of the framework of meanings in the patient's relationship patterns; (2) the CCRT allows the therapist to identify some likely sources of a patient's pain and suffering; (3) the CCRT helps distinguish the positive versus the negative expectations the patient has of others, as well as the patient's typical responses (the positive goals appear to fit with results of analyses of positive goals in the research by Seligman and his colleagues (Seligman, 2002); and (4) the CCRT points to aspects of the relationship theme that need to be mastered.

These reasons for the centrality of the CCRT in supportive-expressive psychotherapy are explained in detail in this book as well as in an earlier book, *Understanding Transference: The Core Conflictual Relationship Theme Method* (Luborsky & Crits-Christoph, 1998).

Principle 7: Use the Symptom-Context Method to Understand the Symptoms

When symptoms emerge in psychotherapy, the Symptom-Context method gives the patient and therapist ways to understand the links between the symptoms and the core issues. This form of expressive work is particularly useful with patients who have disruptive symptoms that seem to be linked to stress, either current stress or post-traumatic stress. When there is a possible medical component to the problem, the patient is advised to see a medical doctor as well.

Principle 8: Encourage Self-Expression, but Avoid Giving Advice

Along with encouraging self-expression, it is typical for the therapist to limit or refrain from giving advice during dynamic psychotherapy (Bibring, 1954). In SE psychotherapy, this is particularly true in treatments weighted toward expressive work.

In fact, in practice there is evidence of much less advice-giving in SE, as compared with other psychotherapies, while there are more nondirective comments from the therapist. Refraining from giving advice helps set up a treatment relationship with the therapist that is less like that of some parents with their children. Instead, it fosters the patients' feeling responsible for making decisions about how to solve their problems.

Principle 9: Individualize the Treatment

SE psychotherapy is made up of supportive and expressive elements, but the mix is specific for each patient. With each new patient, the therapist determines the degree to which the patient needs active support as an element of treatment, as well as the ways the patient may make use of expressive work.

The proportion of each technique and of each response may change as treatment progresses, since the therapist stays in tune with the patient's growth and stays alert to the patient's problems. Each patient brings a unique combination of patterns—both problems and potential. Each psychotherapy reflects both the commonality of the clinical principles and the differences among patients.

Chapter Three

The Essence of SE Session-Limited Psychotherapy

The crucial difference between SE and SE session-limited is the impact of the prearranged limit on the number of sessions and on the patient's motivation in the treatment. That difference brings with it the need for a tighter therapist focus within the sessions.

The practice of SE session-limited has continued to increase. Several practical factors have played a role in that trend: *limited resources*, *limited time*, and the *limits imposed by insurance companies*. These forces are present frequently enough that therapists may find it beneficial to have a working understanding of how a limit on the number of sessions may influence the way they approach the treatment.

For some patients and some therapists, the choice of session-limited treatment is motivated less by practical reasons than by the wish to solve a specific therapeutic problem as efficiently as possible. When a patient has one focal issue but is otherwise functioning well, or when the patient has had a prior treatment and wishes to simply address a current issue, a brief treatment may meet the patient's clinical needs.

In research studies, a time limit can be advantageous in that session-limited treatment makes each treatment a uniform length in terms of the number of sessions. When the patient is actually a subject of a research study, all the parameters of the study, including the length of the treatment offered, need to be clarified with the patient.

SE session-limited psychotherapy fits within the category of short-term, or brief, treatment. All short-term treatments tend to be "focal" treatments, with a central problem as the main topic of treatment, but only SE session-limited uses the Core Conflictual Relationship Theme (CCRT) as the central way to stay in focus. A guide was written specifically for SE time-limited treatment by Book (1998). He describes in detail the use of the CCRT through each phase of the treatment and illustrates how to keep an "empathic therapeutic eye" on the chosen focus.

The research on brief psychotherapy is covered by Koss and Shiang (1994). Other focal therapies include the following: "focal" psychotherapy by Balint, Ornstein, and Balint (1977); "brief" psychotherapy by Malan (1963, 1976); "anxiety-provoking" psychotherapy by Sifneos (1972); "short-term" psychotherapy by Mann (1973); and "time-limited dynamic" psychotherapy by Binder and Strupp (1984, 1991). These time-limited therapies focus with intensity on the problem at hand, with the goal of altering the defenses (Roy, Perry, Luborsky, & Bannon, in press) and thereby solving an underlying problem in a brief time period. They are designed for patients who want to engage in a brief treatment yet luckily have sufficient ego strength to tolerate the anxiety that arises from the brevity of the sessions.

While SE session-limited treatment also tries to accomplish its goals in a brief time, it allows for a supportive element as needed. The treatment can be tolerated by a broad group of patients because the supportive relationship can help diminish the patient's anxiety.

However, research studies on the differences among patient responses to session-limited treatment suggest some caution in its application to patients with serious pathology (Shea, Elkin, & Sotsky, 1999). Certain personality types have been found to respond better to long-term treatment, specifically those who are self-critical and perfectionistic, termed by Blatt "introjective" (Blatt, 1999). These findings highlight the need for an initial evaluation to determine the appropriate treatment for each patient. The initial evaluation may be done either by the therapist or by another member of the treatment or the treatment research team. The forms of evaluation vary from those that include psychological testing or research protocols to those that are done through a clinical interview. The necessary common denominator is for the therapist to determine the overall Health-Sickness level of the patient (Luborsky, Diguer, et al., 1993). The next factor to consider is whether the patient has one focal issue or a number of interwoven problems. Finally, the therapist must consider whether a personality disorder might be present, or highly perfectionistic characteristics, as described already.

Following are the main principles that are most relevant to SE session-limited:

Principle 1: The Short-Term Session Limit Shapes the Treatment

Holding to a session limit has a shaping effect throughout the treatment, meaning that the patient and therapist will keep the focus on the central agenda of the treatment. In each session, the therapist will draw from the material its implications for the patient's central relationship theme and symptoms. Those connections will be brought to light earlier than they might in a longer treatment, often with a more active role played by the therapist in the process.

In SE session-limited psychotherapy, the therapist and patient agree on the number of sessions at the beginning of treatment. Typically, it is less than the 25-session time limit, sometimes with a follow-up of a few additional sessions. Book's (1998) brief therapy model calls for a 16-session limit, for example. The usual SE time-unlimited treatment can sometimes be short term as well, not because of a prearranged decision to limit the number of sessions but, rather, because the needs of the patient call for a limit.

Principle 2: The CCRT Can Provide a Consistent Basis for Interpretations

Near the beginning of SE session-limited psychotherapy, the therapist will determine a central focus for the treatment from the patient's problems and goals. That focus should be on the CCRT and the symptoms connected with it. Or, it may also be on a chosen facet of that theme, one that is most linked to the patient's goals. This means that the therapist and patient will engage in a discovery of the ways the patient's problems are connected to his or her CCRT. The use of the CCRT gives the treatment a kind of self-made map to help look at the patient's relationship patterns within a session-limited frame.

Principle 3: The SE Session-Limited Treatment Type Must Be Appropriate for the Patient's Needs

SE session-limited psychotherapy is particularly suitable for patients who will be living in the locale in which the psychotherapy is given for only a short time, patients with one focal issue who may solve it more efficiently within a session-limited structure, and patients who find the session-limited structure useful for intensifying their efforts to alter defenses and who have the requisite ego strength.

SE session-limited psychotherapy can be beneficial to patients who are well matched to the treatment. In a report of the Treatment of Depression Collaborative Study (Elkin et al., 1989), patients with less serious and less long-standing pathology tended to do better. However, some patients in that study did not respond well to the short-term treatment, probably because of the severity of their diagnosis along with the 12-session time limit (Shea, Elkin,

Imber, & Sotsky, 1992).

Principle 4: SE and SE Session-Limited Psychotherapy Have Similar Basic Treatment Structures

The SE session-limited form of psychotherapy is not an SE that just stops after the chosen number of sessions are completed; rather, it moves through the same basic structure as the usual SE. However, each phase is necessarily more brief and more focused than the usual session-unlimited SE.

The goal of the first phase is to simultaneously develop an initial understanding of the patient's CCRT and to develop a Helping Alliance. In the second phase, the goals are to expand that understanding and link it to the patient's symptoms. The goals of the third, or ending, phase are to help the patient "own" the understanding and to use it for shifts in symptoms and, as much as possible, in the maladaptive components of the CCRT.

Principle 5: Comparisons between Session-Limited and Session-Unlimited Treatment Have Not Yielded Consistent Results

Researchers have made considerable effort to compare the efficacy of short- and long-term treatment, as well as of some studies of session-limited versus session-unlimited treatment. However, the results have not been consistent (Luborsky, 2001).

Seligman's (1995) report for the Consumers Union study noted a greater patient satisfaction with longer-term treatment. A recent comparison of psychoanalysis with psychoanalytic psychotherapy found psychoanalysis to be a more frequent winner (Blomberg, Lazar, & Sandell, 2001). Extrapolating from recent studies, it is likely that comparisons will eventually show that longer psychotherapy tends toward better outcomes.

Principle 6: A Strong "Helping Alliance" Should Be Forged

During each session, the therapist needs to make responses that strengthen the Helping Alliance. The patient and therapist need a strong partnership to accomplish their goals in a brief time period. The therapist needs to keep an eye on the state of the alliance and must address any problems that may emerge.

Although SE session-limited treatment requires more focus on the central themes, it does not mean that the therapist's empathy for the patient's experience should be so limited. The therapist's willingness to stay open to the patient's responses, especially when they are not in line with the therapist's thinking, keeps the treatment true to the patient. When the therapist conveys empathy for the patient's emotional experience, it strengthens the

Helping Alliance.

EXAMPLE 1: Mr. Charles H. Montgomery

P: I don't want to be another Woody Allen, spending my life whining on a couch. I just want to get this over with.

Background: In the initial evaluation session, the patient revealed he had been in therapy before. He explained that he "got somewhere" because he used to quit jobs—because of "fear of commitment"—and after a while he began to realize he had been "wasting time" by his precipitous changes.

T: So what brings you back?

P: They are laying people off all around me. I finally got so I could stay with a job. [With some pride] I've been there 6 years, but it doesn't look so good. . . ."

T: So, you are finally able to stay with a job, but then things started changing around you.

P: [Looks up] Yeah. [Pause] It kind of makes me nervous, I have to say. . . . And, well, I met this woman on a ski trip, and I, um, might want to do it. . . .

T: Might want to actually stay with this person?

P: [Looks up again] You got it.

The therapist evaluated the level of pathology and found that although the patient had a history of episodes of anxiety and impulsivity, he was able to function in daily life despite his symptoms.

The therapist also felt that the patient was accurate when he said he "got somewhere" in the previous treatment, since he was currently at another level with his fears and functioning. He wondered if the patient's wish for a brief treatment was because his "fear of commitment" that was not entirely resolved. That could mean that choosing a session-limited treatment would be a way to limit his commitment. However, the therapist also felt that the patient could use a brief treatment to keep an active focus on that problem. The therapist decided to let the decision be the patient's after presenting his thoughts on the ways each decision might affect the treatment.

EXAMPLE 2: Ms. Julie M. Sandberg

P: How many times am I supposed to come here?

T: Tell me your thoughts about that. Maybe we can figure it out together.

P: Well, I wasn't sure about this whole therapy thing. My friend suggested it. The only way I got myself in the door was to tell myself I didn't have to come back if I didn't like it.

T: So you got yourself to open the door that way.

P: And now I don't know what to think. Anyway, I can't really afford it. So better keep it short.

T: [Makes a mental note of a possible CCRT theme: The patient is saying that she thinks of cutting off the experience to protect herself from whatever might go wrong if she engages in the therapy. However, she says only one part of that.]

T: I wonder if it felt scary to start talking here.

P: Well, so far it's been better than I thought, but, you know [falls silent and looks at her lap], if I go into it more, I don't know. [Patient looks tense.]

T: Sounds like you are worried about things going wrong. Has that happened much in your life?

P: [Bites her lip] That's for sure.

Background: After exploring the foreground as well as the background, the therapist discovered that the patient, a young woman in her late 20s, had had several episodes of depression, each of them linked to breakups with boyfriends or other forms of loss. Right now she is "trying not to get depressed" after her boyfriend decided they should "take a break and see other people."

The therapist reached the conclusion that a time-limited treatment would not be in the patient's best interests. With both a history of depression and a vulnerability to loss, she thought that the patient would be unlikely to tolerate a fixed length. Instead, the therapist believed that the patient's fears of something going wrong should be explored without a time limit, "So we can get to the point where things go right," she explained to the patient. They then discussed the fee, making an adjustment that felt acceptable to the patient and to the therapist.

SUMMARY AND DISCUSSION

Session-limited SE has fundamental similarities to open-ended SE psychotherapy. Both follow the principle for SE described in this manual: The patient and therapist are more attentive to the passage of time and consequently stay more focused on a core issue. Session-limited SE has similarities to the broader description of brief psychotherapy in that it is a focal therapy (Koss & Shiang, 1994).

Session-limited SE has a few other advantages over the usual open-ended SE psychotherapy. The following are the most obvious advantages:

1. The treatment takes relatively little time.
2. The treatment length is conveniently predictable.
3. SE session-limited treatment has an advantage if the patient has only a short time to remain in a locale accessible to the treatment. It is also beneficial to patients who have one central issue to resolve, including those who have already had a longer treatment but are returning to resolve a new issue of, for example, firming up previous gains.
4. For some, it can be a safely constructed first step toward self-understanding. For others, it may be a way to efficiently solve the problems at hand.
5. The time limit can also make the patient feel an acceptable pressure to

change in a short period of time. Such treatment limits can leave less time to modulate the expressive work with supportive elements. For that reason, the match of patient with technique should be made cautiously. For patients who do not experience the time limit as undue pressure, the urgency of the time limit can increase the central change agents, with the focus on the CCRT as a guide.

6. Yet many patients cannot get to the heart of their problems in a brief period of time. Some have complex, interwoven problems that cannot be unraveled quickly. There are also patients who do not establish trust easily, those who are highly self-critical and perfectionistic (Shahar, Blatt, Zuroff, & Pilkonis, 2003), and those who cannot tolerate anxiety well. All these patients are better served by a session-unlimited treatment.

Following are recommendations for doing SE session-limited psychotherapy:

1. Select patients who are willing and able to accept a brief treatment.
2. Evaluate the patient's overall Health-Sickness level, as well as the ability to tolerate anxiety and tendencies toward self-criticism.
3. Establish treatment goals and work actively toward those goals.
4. Evaluate and nurture when necessary the development of a Helping Alliance; keep alert to signs ruptures in the alliance, and work to resolve them as they emerge.
5. Keep the therapeutic focus around the CCRT.
6. Get the patient ready to end the treatment by summarizing the discoveries and by exploring what termination means to the patient. Work through those concerns, and emphasize the gains from the treatment.

PART II

CLINICAL RESEARCH METHODS

Chapter Four

The Core Conflictual Relationship Theme (CCRT) Method

Long before the Core Conflictual Relationship Theme (CCRT) method was conceived, dynamic therapists had an interest in uncovering problematic patterns in patients' relationships. These patterns often led to unsatisfying relationships, to symptoms, or to both. Now we have the first reliable system for guiding the therapist to formulate relationship patterns—the CCRT (Luborsky, 1997). The CCRT is recommended for use with SE psychotherapy because it brings clarity to a previously unguided clinical process. But that clinical process has not been simply guesswork. It involves a process of pattern recognition that takes training and skill. What exactly are seasoned therapists doing when they listen for such patterns?

It is not enough to explain that "one listens and the understanding comes," as I relearned from a psychiatrist in training (Perry Berman) whom I supervised many years ago. He played a part in my realization by adding: "There must be more to the process of learning the main relationship theme than you have been telling me. You should spell out the principles guiding your understanding." In time I did exactly that, and I came up with the principles for the CCRT, as explained in this book, which were then tested through research.

THE FUNCTION OF THE CCRT

The CCRT can be defined as the repeating pattern a person follows when conducting relationships. In order to discern the CCRT, the therapist or researcher listens for the repeated themes in the narratives the patient tells during sessions, themes composed of the patient's wishes, the responses of others, and how he responds himself. The responses from others include both real responses and anticipated responses. Sometimes the patient's narrative suggests that he may be responding to an expectation of which he is not actively aware. Having the CCRT in mind can help the therapist listen for or inquire about an implied expectation. That helps the patient begin to separate expectations from reality.

The therapist or researcher listens for and rates these three central elements: the patient's wish (W), the actual response or anticipated response from others (RO), and the response of the self (RS). The nature and themes of those three elements form the essential structure of each patient's CCRT.

Common examples of a CCRT include the following:

WISH (W): To be loved
RESPONSE FROM OTHERS (RO): Rejection
RESPONSE OF SELF (RS): Avoidance

WISH (W): To be recognized or to feel important
RESPONSE FROM OTHERS (RO): No recognition
RESPONSE OF SELF (RS): Anger or angry behavior

The CCRT is often embedded in the patient's narrative, in stories of her encounters with others, as well as in her reactions to life events. Listening for the CCRT is like tracking a red thread across a field, an analogy used by another resident I supervised years ago, Ellen Berman. The red thread corresponds to the patient's central relationship pattern, as estimated by the CCRT. The therapist keeps an eye out for the "red thread" in the material the patient brings so that the patient and therapist can decode it together.

THE CCRT AND THE TRANSFERENCE PATTERN

The CCRT can be thought of as an operational version of essential principles of the transference, Freud's (1912a/1958) cornerstone psychoanalytic concept. Freud gave this description of the concept:

> "Each individual, through the combined operation of his innate disposition and the influences brought to bear on him during his early years, has acquired a specific method of his own in the conduct of his erotic life. This produces a stereotype plate (or several such) which is constantly repeated . . . in the course of the person's life." (pp. 99-100)

How much evidence is there that the CCRT corresponds to Freud's concept of the transference? Does it maintain the central functions that he described? We examined these questions in detail and came up with striking results. We found 23 qualities that were closely associated with the concept described in

Freud (1912a/1958). We correlated 18 of Freud's 23 observations with the CCRT and found a high concordance between the two. We then divided these correspondences into eight central qualities of the transference that can be found in the CCRT (as listed in table 4.1 and described in greater detail in Luborsky and Crits-Christoph, 1998). These results suggest that the CCRT does indeed function as a measure of essential qualities of what Freud described as the "transference pattern."

Table 4.1. Correspondence of the CCRT with the Transference Pattern

Result 1: The CCRT is pervasive across narratives about different people, and it maintains its pervasiveness late in treatment as well.
Result 2: The CCRT has a strong positive and strong negative dimension that can be reliably scored. It changes in treatment in a way that is significant and clinically meaningful.
Result 3: Our studies show that the CCRT has a parallel pattern for the relationship with the therapist, the relationship with others, and the relationship with the self.
Result 4: The pattern is similar in both dreams and narratives.
Result 5: Accuracy of interpretation was linked to outcome, in particular with the accuracy of responses about the wish plus the response from others plus the response of self.
Result 6: The CCRT exists before treatment, as evidenced by Barber, Luborsky, Crits-Christoph, and Diguer (1995). This study shows a parallel between the CCRT before treatment starts, and the CCRT patterns in the early sessions of the treatment.
Result 7: A study of CCRT patterns in young children shows stability from age 3 to age 5; considerable study of early attachment patterns also shows stability over time.
Result 8: The parallel between the CCRT and the general transference template was confirmed, with correspondences found for 18 of 23 of Freud's 1912 observations.

WORKING WITH THE CCRT DURING A SESSION

The CCRT provides a framework for listening to what the patient tends to expect from himself and from others. These patterns can be noticed through both the relationship episodes (REs) the patient tells during sessions and the ways the patient responds to the therapist. The therapist listens for the main repeated themes in the narratives the patient tells spontaneously during sessions. Patients typically tell an average of four such relationship episode narratives in each session (Francis et al., in preparation).

Once the therapist has attuned his ear to hear REs, he is ready to listen for what they are made of. As the concrete definition of the CCRT, it is made up of the top frequencies of the three central elements: the wish (W), the response from others (RO), and the response of the self (RS). These elements can be thought of as three strands of the "red thread" of the CCRT.

Each element can also be scored as positive (P) or negative (N). These elements may either be present or implied in any relationship episode. The clinical assessment of the CCRT may be done *during* a session; the CCRT may also be assessed *after* a session by the rating of a transcription of the REs of the session.

In tracking the three elements of the CCRT, the therapist or researcher is essentially tracking the fate of "the wish." The patient's narratives will include a sense of what he really wishes for, either implied or directly expressed. Common wishes include the wish to be close, to be loved, to be independent, or to assert one's self. As true to the name of the central pattern, Core *Conflictual* Relationship Theme, the responses of self and others are often at odds with the patient's wish.

The patient frequently experiences or anticipates some form of negative responses from others—perhaps rejection or criticism. The response of self often includes its own negative pattern, including anxiety, or a form of defense, such as avoidance (Roy, Perry, Luborsky, & Bannon, in preparation).

THE ROLE OF THE CCRT IN SE PSYCHOTHERAPY

In highlighting different elements of the CCRT, the therapist and patient have their eyes on what happens to what the patient wishes for himself. After the therapist has helped make it clear, the patient may begin to notice the CCRT pattern on his own. That awareness of the existence of the pattern allows the patient to begin to move toward the next phase of CCRT work: making changes in his habitual pattern.

Working through the CCRT pattern means that a pattern that was once second nature becomes a process to notice and to question. A gradual shift in the negative expectations from others and maladaptive personal responses can emerge in the later phases of the work (see chapter 12). In fact, CCRT research suggests that after a successful treatment, the patient's wishes remain consistent, while the negative responses from self and others undergo change (Levine & Luborsky, 1981; Luborsky & Crits-Christoph, 1998).

LEARNING THE CCRT METHOD

The therapist will want to practice enough so that the CCRT method can be used with ease, especially *during* the session. When used in research, raters will need to practice the method enough to achieve interrater reliability.

A good way to get practice in using the CCRT is by reviewing a sample of the relationship episodes in the patient's narratives because REs give concrete examples of personally meaningful episodes in dealings with other people. For purposes of formulating the CCRT, it is helpful to rely on interactions with other people, including with the therapist. A scored example of Mr. Edward Howard is presented here in a form that gives an example of the scoring process:

EXAMPLE: Mr. Edward Howard

In this example of Mr. Howard, we will rely on a presentation in three parts: (1) a brief case summary, (2) a list of the REs found in Session 3, and (3) a brief summary of the CCRT itself in that session.

A Brief Case Summary

When he started treatment, Mr. Howard, then 20 years old, had begun his third year of college. He came for psychotherapy with these symptoms and problems: anxiety, guilt, sporadic pain in the penis, difficulty in dealing with a new girlfriend, and resentment of his parents. He had never felt close to his father, but felt very close to his mother.

During the first two months of treatment, the patient's passivity and difficulty in relationships became increasingly evident. His CCRT, as illustrated during the transcript given in box 4.1, illustrates the inner workings of his relationship and self-esteem difficulties.

RE 1: Mother NRO: Disagrees with his view (8, 14) W: To get sexual information (8?, 11?) (W): To get close to M. (11?, 8) PRO: (past) Explains (11, 13) NRO: Rejects (4, 12) NRS: Frustration (21, 20?) NRS: Shame (26, 25)	//This might have been a dream.//[RO]Mother says it didn't happen.//[W,(W)]Up until we moved, when I had questions about sex,//[RO]mother would explain.//When we moved to ___, one day I asked and //[RO]she said, "Sorry we can't talk about that. You're getting to that age."//[RS]Bothered me 'cause my young sister, age 9 or 10, laughed.//
RE 2: Mother NRO: Disagrees with his view (8, 14) PRO: (past) Closeness (11?, 13?) (W): To be physically close (11, 8?) NRO: Rejection, choose someone else (4, 12)	//[RO]Another incident mother said never happened.//[RO,(W)]We, brother and I before sister was born, when it was really cold, would sleep with my parents.//[RO]Parents took my brother in bed with them and they wouldn't take me.
RE 3: Therapist NRS: Unresponsive, distant (8, 16) NRS: Headache (31?) NRS: Tense (27, 19?) NRS: Lack of response on his part (8, 16?) NRO: No rapport (12, 14?) NRS: Lack of response on his part (8, 16?)	T: What's happening now? P: //[RS]I feel generally unresponsive.//[RS]I'm getting a headache,//[RS]tense,//[RS]thinking all week about relating all this stuff to what I was 10 years ago [sigh] and not getting any—I mean, nothing comes out//. . . like groups of guys who have embarrassing moments of silence.//[RO]It proves no perfect rapport exists.//[RS]I feel blank.
RE 4: Mother (W): To be close, have affection (11, 7) PRS: (past) Closeness, affection (30, 5) NRO: Blames (4, 27) NRS: Felt alone (23, 20?)	//[(W),RS]Before I went to school, I always used to kiss my mother.//I'm not sure it was a big thing, but it was a big thing when it stopped.//[RO]She made a big thing about how I didn't want to kiss her anymore.//[RS]I was suddenly out in the cold again.

RE 5: Girlfriend: E.	
NRS: Resentment (21, 20?)	//[RS]I'm beginning to feel a lot of resentment to E. [girlfriend].//[(W)]I went with her for a couple of years.//[RO]It's just been severed.//[RS]I'm fearful of seeing her and feeling something for her.//[RO]She just doesn't give a damn.//[RS]Bothers me I used to be so screwed up about her.//
(W): To not suffer loss of rel. (11?, 33?)	
NRO: Cuts off rel. (4, 14?)	
NRS: Fear of wish for attachment (19?, 27?)	
NRO: Rejects (4?, 15)	
NRS: Blames self (25, 17)	
RE 6: Mother	
NRS: Resentment (21, 11?)	//[RS]One thing that started my resentment against my parents.//[(W)]I told her about E. [girlfriend], that everything was cut off.//I said E.'s not writing and it upset me.//[RO]She said, "Well, I'm sure about you and you aren't sure about her."//That really cut me up//[RO]because of the rel . . . relationship she . . . she . . . a . . . assumes between us is like between E. and me.//
(W): To not be cut off from girlfriend (11, 14?)	
NRO: Hurts P. (15, 4)	
NRO: Assumes P. loves girl like he loves his mother—a hurtful idea to him (2, 15)	

Box 4.1. CCRT Transcript

Mr. Edward Howard: CCRT Scoring [condensed] from Session 3 (Luborsky & Crits-Christoph, 1998)

Scoring the CCRT

The RE narratives were first divided by the scorer into thought units for scoring in the usual manner after a session was completed and transcribed. The REs may be scored either by tailor-made or standard categories for the CCRT elements. Tailor-made categories are derived by the judges, while standard categories, which can be found in appendix A, identify common wishes and responses. Edition 2 of the standard categories (Crits-Christoph & Demorest, 1988) were used in this case example. Since that time, we have developed a subsequent version, Edition 3, which reduces redundancy through cluster analysis. Table 4.2 shows the scoring for both of those systems.

When working with the standard categories, choose the scores that best reflect the thought unit; these are the first most-fitting and the second most-fitting choices. In this case, wish number 11 (to be close to others) was judged as most frequent, with wish number 8 (to be opened up to) as second most frequent.

The first step in evaluating the results is a count of the number of scores among the REs that are scored for each of the main components. The first result is for the wish (W) score. In five out of the six REs in session three, the wish to be close (number 11) was prominent. The next result is the response from others (RO). The most frequent response, "are rejecting" (number 4), occurred four times, while the second most frequent response, "are not trustworthy" (number 8), occurred twice. The third result is the response of self (RS). The most frequent response, "feel angry" (number 21), occurred three times, while seven other negative responses occurred once.

The scoring in this example of a session also includes the number of negative (N) and positive (P) scores. For these six REs, the negatives are far greater than the positives, a finding that is frequent in patient populations. In this sample,

Table 4.2. Standard Categories for Scoring the CCRT components

Edition 3 (clusters)	*Edition 2*
WISHES	
1. To assert self and be independent	21. To have self-control
	28. To be my own person
	34. To assert myself
	23. To be independent
2. To oppose, hurt, and control others	18. To oppose others
	16. To hurt others
	19. To have control of others
3. To be controlled, hurt, and not responsible	15. To be hurt
	20. To be controlled by others
	29. To not be responsible/obligated
	13. To be helped
	27. To be like others
4. To be distant and avoid conflicts	17. To avoid conflicts
	14. To not be hurt
	10. To be distant from others
5. To be close and accepting	4. To accept others
	5. To respect others
	9. To be open
	6. To have trust
	8. To be opened up to
	11. To be close to others
6. To be loved and understood	33. To be loved
	3. To be respected
	1. To be understood
	2. To be accepted
	7. To be liked
7. To feel good and comfortable	30. To have stability
	31. To feel comfortable
	32. To feel happy
	24. To feel good about self
8. To achieve and help others	22. To achieve
	25. To better myself
	12. To help others
	26. To be good
RESPONSES FROM OTHER	
1. Strong	24. Strong
	23. Independent
	29. Happy
2. Controlling	26. Strict
	20. Controlling

Continued

Table 4.2. ***(Continued)***

Edition 3 (clusters)	Edition 2
3. Upset	16. Hurt 22. Dependent 28. Anxious 27. Anger 19. Out of control
4. Bad	8. Not trustworthy 25. Bad
5. Rejecting and opposing	7. Don't trust me 6. Don't respect me 2. Are not understanding 4. Rejecting 10. Dislike me 12. Distant 14. Unhelpful 17. Oppose me 15. Hurt me
6. Helpful	13. Are helpful 18. Cooperative
7. Likes me	30. Loves me 5. Respects me 9. Likes me 21. Gives me independence
8. Understanding	11. Open 1. Understanding 3. Accepting
RESPONSES OF SELF	
1. Helpful	7. Am open 1. Understand 9. Am helpful
2. Unreceptive	2. Don't understand 8. Am not open 6. Dislike others
3. Respected and accepted	28. Feel comfortable 29. Feel happy 30. Feel loved 4. Feel respected 3. Feel accepted 5. Like others
4. Oppose and hurt others	11. Oppose others 10. Hurt others

Table 4.2. *(Continued)*

Edition 3 (clusters)	*Edition 2*
5. Self-controlled and self-confident	14. Self-controlled 15. Independent 18. Self-confident 12. Controlling
6. Helpless	13. Out of control 17. Helpless 19. Uncertain 16. Dependent
7. Disappointed and depressed	21. Angry 20. Disappointed 22. Depressed 23. Unloved 24. Jealous
8. Anxious and ashamed	27. Anxious 26. Ashamed 25. Guilty

there are 20 negatives and only 3 positives, a ratio heavily in favor of the negatives.

The CCRT emerges from the highest frequency of the scoring of each element in the session. Here are the results of Mr. Howard's CCRT pattern:
Wish (W): "I want to be close to others."
Response from others (RO): "The other rejects me."
Response of self (RS): "I feel rejected and become angry."

STEPS IN ASSESSING THE CCRT AFTER THE SESSION AND FROM THE TRANSCRIPT

This procedure gives a more complete assessment of the CCRT than the *in-session* approach. It is utilized when doing research with the CCRT. It is also useful for clinicians who are learning how to become fluent in the CCRT method.

Step 1: Finding and Identifying Relationship Episodes (REs)

1. *Finding REs:* The first step when scoring *after* the session is completed is to mark the places in the transcript where descriptions of specific events are given. This is a crucial step because the CCRT is defined in terms of

such relationship episodes (REs). Most REs are about specific interactions, either real or imagined. The location of the RE need only be identified once (i.e., by the first judge who is assigned to review the session); the other judges can then use the location noted by the original judge.

2. *Marking the length of each RE:* Mark the beginning and ending of the RE on the left margin of the transcript. At the beginning of the RE, put the RE numbers in sequence. The narratives of the RE are marked off by an independent judge by a line on the left margin from the beginning to the end of the account of the episode. Also on the left margin at the beginning of the line, the central other person in the RE is identified.
3. *Rating the completeness of the narrative:* At the beginning of the RE, rate its completeness. "Completeness" is the amount of detail in the narrative on a 1 to 5 scale from "very little" to "very much" for each of the three CCRT components (W, RO, RS). A usual rating of completeness of 2.5 (on a 5-point scale) qualifies an RE for its possible inclusion in the CCRT (Luborsky, 1984).
4. *Picking the main other person:* At the beginning of the RE, identify the main other person with whom the self interacts and is therefore discussed most in the RE (e.g., mother, father, brother, sister). There may be more than one other person in an RE, but only the main one is selected, and that choice of person is usually an easy selection.
5. *Identifying and then scoring the thought units in the narratives to be CCRT scored:* A thought unit is a possible complete thought. Mark off with double slashes the thought units in each of the REs that are to be scored. The type of component that should be scored is noted above the start of the thought unit, as suggested by Benjamin (1994). Each thought is given two specific scores: the best-fitting score and the next-best-fitting score. Independent studies of the judge's agreement on these two steps are moderate—they are higher for the most fitting than the next most fitting, with the first significantly higher than the second (Francis et al., in preparation).
6. *Scoring each of the thought units:* Rate both the most-fitting and the next-most-fitting thought unit from the scoring lists for wishes (W), responses from others (RO), and responses of self (RS).
7. *Dropping duplicate thought units:* In summing the scored components for each RE, count only one *duplicate* thought unit—duplicates are complete and immediate repetitions of prior ones just scored.

Step 2: Guide for Scoring Wishes (W)

The judge reads the transcript with the REs located in it and scores two kinds of wish (W): (1) those that are explicit and (2) those from which the CCRT components can be inferred. If the wish is not even moderately inferable, no W score is given. In the following case of Mr. Tom Mooney, his primary wish, to make a commitment, could be inferred.

EXAMPLE: Mr. Tom Mooney

The CCRT judge was not sure which of Mr. Mooney's two wishes was primary—Wish 1: "I want to make a commitment to a person or to a job, but it makes me feel too trapped" or Wish 2: "I want to avoid making a commitment to a person or to a job, but I am under strong pressure to make such a commitment." The question for the judge was whether the wish to make or the wish to avoid making a commitment was the primary wish. Usually there is a greater frequency of one of the wishes. In fact, with Mr. Tom Mooney, there was evidence that there was first an urge to make a commitment, then the feeling of being trapped, and then a further wish to avoid making a commitment—the frequency and the prior position in the sequence of the wish to make a commitment led it to be scored as the primary wish.

The example just given illustrates a trend—the tendency for positive wishes to be primary. It sounds as if this could be a reflection of the judge's values, but it seems more likely to be the case that people who enter psychotherapy are striving toward positive goals.

Step 3: Guide for Scoring Responses from Others (RO)

The ROs tend to be easier to score than the Ws since they are more directly expressed. There is no requirement that the scorer be able to see the responses as related to a particular wish; it is sufficient for the scorer to note all wishes and note all responses without having to connect each of the responses to each of the wishes.

Step 4: Guide for Scoring Responses of Self (RS)

All responses of self are included, as in the listing of the categories. Responses of the self include both verbalizations and behavior.

Step 5: "Expressed" versus "Considered" Responses (optional)

The subscript *exp* meaning *expressed* or *con* meaning *considered* can be applied to either an RO or an RS. An example of an RS_{con} can be found in Mr. Bruce Norwood's reaction in step 7 ("That made me angry"). This comment is merely a *considered* response because the patient makes it clear that he did not *express* his irritation to the other person. On the other hand, the other person did express the wish to dominate him; therefore, the scoring is RO_{EXP}. The distinction between expressed and considered is of particular value in studying the CCRT as a measure of change during psychotherapy.

Step 6: Positive and Negative Responses (optional)

Each type of response may be further subdivided into a major dichotomy: mainly positive (P) responses or mainly negative (N) responses. By far the most common type of response in most groups is negative, defined as a response that means to the patient that an interference with satisfaction of wishes has occurred or is expected to occur. In contrast, a positive response refers to a noninterference or expectation of noninterference with the satisfaction of wishes or a sense of mastery in being able to deal with the wishes.

Step 7: Intensity of Theme Components (optional)

Theme components vary in their intensity. A scale from 1 to 5 may be sufficient for grading the intensity of each type of component, as noted in the following example.

EXAMPLE: Mr. Bruce R. Norwood

	Score	Intensity Rating
"I wish to assert myself."	(W)	4
"He dominated by not letting me speak."	RO	4
"I was angry."	RS	5

Step 8: Guide for Scoring the Patient's Experience of the Relationship (optional)

According to the psychoanalytic theory of psychotherapeutic change, patients in treatment should gain improved awareness of their experience in relationships, including the relationship with the therapist. The CCRT scoring of a session, since it often encompasses the interactions with the therapist, reflects the patient's experience of the relationship.

In order to study this dimension, more precise scoring distinctions about the awareness of qualities of interpersonal experiences are needed. These should include the degree to which each component of the CCRT is consciously experienced and the degree of awareness of the experience in the relationship with the therapist. Also needed is a distinction between degrees of awareness of the parallels between experience in the session versus outside the session, as put forward by Gill and Hoffman (1982). The scoring distinctions are mostly similar to those included in Gill's (1979, 1982) method of coding a PERT (a patient's experience of the relationship with the therapist): the degree to which the component is experienced in the relationship to the therapist (Gill's "r") (Gill & Hoffman, 1982, p. 148), the degree to which the patient is aware of the experience in the relationship with the therapist (this is our label "ra"), and the degree to which the patient is aware of the parallel between the relationship with the therapist and relationships outside of treatment (Gill's "xr" and "rx") (Gill & Hoffman, 1982, p. 149). Also, a judge may infer that there is an implicit allusion to the patient's experience of the relationship in communications that are not manifestly about the relationship (Gill's "Jxr")(Gill & Hoffman, 1982, p. 149).

Step 9: Three Principles of Abstract Inference-Making (optional)

Now that concrete principles for understanding the patient's main communications have been discussed, it is of interest and value to stand back and see some of the more abstract principles that assist the clinician in making inferences. The following are the three most reliable and most used abstract principles:

1. ***The redundancy:*** This principle is easy to overlook, since redundancy often causes people to pay less attention. However, redundancy can provide a clue to the importance of a theme. Inspecting the contexts in their sequence allows recognition of significant redundancies in the components of relationship episodes. The frequency of a particular response may be evident in different spheres of a patient's life. A detailed example of this kind of redundancy is provided in chapter 10, in which the patient (Peter Quinn) conveys feelings of inadequacy in different situations.
2. ***The temporal contiguity:*** Temporal contiguity gives another way to gather the data for understanding. This principle means that when two thoughts follow each other, they may have a causal link. Also, the more often they follow each other, the more likely there is a causal link. In other words, the emotional importance of the theme is causing the patient to put the two topics together. The temporal contiguity may be between successive thoughts or within each of the sequential components of the typical Symptom-Context sequence: (1) presymptom, (2) symptom, and (3) postsymptom, as shown in Luborsky (1996).
3. ***The shifts in mental state:*** The workings of a psychological system tend to be more clearly seen during its shifts than during its stasis. This principle is evident in the examples of depressive mood shifts (Luborsky, Singer, Hartke, Diguer, Crits-Christoph, & Peterson, 1996) and in the method by Horowitz, Marmar, and Wilner (1979) and Horowitz (1979) for

analyzing shifts in state during psychotherapy. The theme that immediately preceded the shift is likely to contain clues to the problem, as may changes in affect. The Symptom-Context method provides a powerful tool for understanding such shifts in state (chapter 5).

SUMMARY OF NOTATIONS FOR SCORING THE RELATIONSHIP EPISODES (RE) FOR THE CCRT

Step 1: Relationship Episodes
RE = relationship episode
RE*c* = current RE
RE*p* = past and early-in-life RE

Steps 2, 3, 4: The CCRT Method
W = wish, as directly stated by the patient
(W) = wish, as inferred by the judge
RO = response from the main other person
RS = response of the self

Step 5: Expressed Versus Considered Responses (optional)
exp = expressed response to the other person (e.g., NRS_{exp} = negative response from self that is expressed)
con = considered response not expressed to the other person

Step 6: Positive and Negative Responses (optional)
N = negative (e.g., NRO = negative response from the other)
P = positive

Step 7: Intensity of Theme Components (optional)
A 1 to 5 rating of the intensity of each theme component (W, RO, RS)

Step 8: Patient's Experience of the Relationship (optional)
r = experienced in the relationship with the therapist in the session
ra = aware of being experienced in the relationship with the therapist in the session
xr and rx = aware of the parallel between relationship with the therapist and outside relationships (x)
Jxr and Jrx = inference by the judge of a parallel between the relationship to T and outside relationships, from communications that are not manifestly about the relationship

THE CCRT AND OTHER RELATIONSHIP SCHEMAS

The CCRT was the first method for deriving relationship theme formulations from psychotherapy that could be used in research (Luborsky, 1976, 1977). Since its invention, more than a dozen somewhat similar methods for discerning objective relationship pattern formulations have followed, as described in Luborsky and Crits-Christoph (1998).

A near relative of the CCRT method is a coding scheme for evaluating the patient's experience of the relationship with the therapist (PERT) (Gill & Hoffman, 1982). The scoring scheme for the PERT catches both direct and indirect references to the relationship of the patient and therapist; this division roughly corresponds to whether the connections are made explicit by the patient, the therapist, or the observer. A second system used to formulate the patient's "unconscious plan," based on a clinical evaluation of the early sessions of psychotherapy by a group of clinicians, is an even nearer relative (Weiss & Sampson, 1986).

A SAMPLE OF RECENT CCRT RESEARCH RESULTS

Consistency of the CCRT from Pretreatment to Early in Psychotherapy

Barber, Luborsky, Crits-Christoph, and Diguer (1995) indicate that the CCRT has an existence apart from suggestion by the therapist. This is demonstrated by the consistency of the CCRT from narratives told prior to psychotherapy to those conveyed early in psychotherapy.

Discovery of the Underlying Brain Location of the CCRT Activity

The activation of the underlying brain location of CCRT activity has now been recorded through the fMRI (Loughead et al., in preparation). This study is the first to look at the neurologic basis of CCRT processing. It offers a way to see brain processing while the CCRT is actually "in mind." Greater brain activation was found when subjects read their own CCRT narratives than when they were in the control condition of reading the CCRTs of others. Increased inferior frontal and thalamic activity, as well as increased activity in the occipital and temporal areas, was found during the reading of their own CCRTs.

Reliability: Agreement on the CCRT by Correlating the Usual RE Method with the RAP (Relationship Anecdotes Paradigms) Method

The usual method for collecting narratives for the CCRT, known as the RE method, is based on psychotherapy sessions containing narratives told *spontaneously*. In contrast, the newer method, the RAP method, is based on *requested* narratives. We have studied the correlation between the RAP method and the RE method, as suggested by Robert Rosenthal (Francis et al., in preparation). We found that the narratives collected by each method changed to a similar extent from the beginning to the end of treatment. This suggests that the two methods were operating similarly, with both methods able to discern the change in the CCRT that occurs in treatment.

Reliability: Agreement on the CCRT Measured at Certain Outcome Points

In a treatment that is benefiting the patient, there are both major consistencies and distinct changes in the CCRT from the start to the end of treatment. Not only does a partly new CCRT appear, but the CCRT also shows changes that fit with the goals of treatment. Here is an example:

EXAMPLE: Ms. Cindy Frank

In the previous session, the patient had become angry at the man she was dating because he kept dropping his fork on the floor during dinner. She felt that was a reflection of disrespect for her. In fact, the patient has again and again over the years gotten angry at anything she interprets as unfairness or disrespect from a man and exploded with anger in ways that destroyed the relationship.

In this session, however, she reported that she was able to recall that the therapist suggested in a recent session that there might be other ways to interpret the man's dropping of his fork, which helped her reconsider her reaction. In the present session, she reported that she had gotten angry at a teacher's unfairness in altering the patient's teaching schedule, but instead of her usual explosion of anger to put the man down, she was able to give herself a pause to think it over. This time the pause allowed her to think of asking the man's secretary what had in fact happened. What she learned made her realize that there had been no sign of disrespect, so she was able to cope with it in a reasonable fashion. The patient sized up this change in her response as large, which it was.

In this treatment, the changes in the RO and RS were impressive—she changed during the treatment in her RO and RS from mostly negative at the beginning to mostly positive by the termination (Luborsky & Crits-Christoph, 1998).

Inexperienced CCRT Scorers versus Experienced CCRT Scorers

Our aim here is to offer guidance to those who select CCRT judges (Luborsky, Diguer, et al., 2004). We compared agreement by multiple scorers for two cases assessed by CCRT-inexperienced judges with two cases assessed by CCRT-experienced judges. Overall, we found at least moderate agreement from the CCRT scoring of the two sample cases by each judge.

However, the judges' amount of experience in scoring the CCRT played an important part in the level of agreement they achieved. The CCRT-inexperienced judges agreed with the larger set of CCRT-experienced judges with a kappa of .58 (mean); but the more CCRT-experienced judges agreed with other judges about .70 (mean). We therefore conclude that the CCRT for all its *apparent* complexity is not difficult to learn, even for CCRT-inexperienced judges—the CCRT-inexperienced judges showed a fair agreement, but the CCRT-experienced judges agreed significantly well with each other.

Reliability: Agreement of the CCRT on Reliability of Scoring

Agreement of judges on the CCRT measure is a large part of reliability. Luborsky and Crits-Christoph (1998) measured the mean for a summary of eight different studies, finding moderate weighted kappas with a mean for each of the three components: W = .60, RO = .68, and RS = .71.

This indicates a high level of interjudge reliability, particularly for the responses from others and responses of self, which typically need less inference by the judge. However, this type of analysis should be redone both for another sample and by another *correlational* method (as proposed by Robert Rosenthal) in Francis et al. (in preparation).

SUMMARY AND DISCUSSION

The CCRT has been increasingly used over the past 28 years as an objective measure of the central relationship pattern. It is justified to call the CCRT a measure of the transference because it fits with most of Freud's (1912a/1958) observations about transference (Luborsky, McLellan, Woody, O'Brien, & Auerbach, 1985; Luborsky & Crits-Christoph, 1998). In fact, the CCRT method was the first clinical-quantitative measure in the field of psychology that is similar to the content of the transference pattern. This theory of psychotherapy assumes that it is the reexperiencing and working through of the recurrent relationship pattern that is the central change agent in psychotherapy.

Consequently, the CCRT is a method that can add reliability to the interpretation process in dynamic psychotherapy. The CCRT allows the concept of transference to be studied by clinical research. It brings the potential for further understanding of intrapsychic processes and interpersonal experiences. The recent discovery of a method of establishing the brain location of CCRT activity allows its neurologic basis to be explored (Loughead et al., in preparation). A summary of the research on the CCRT can be found in many places, including Levine and Luborsky (1981); Luborsky and Crits-Christoph (1998); and Luborsky, Diguer, Kaechele, et al. (1999), as well as in this book.

Chapter Five

The Symptom-Context Method

When a symptom appears in the course of a psychotherapy session, it is as if an astronomer finds himself in the midst of a display of shooting stars. It brings to the therapist a natural opportunity to try to understand the context and the conditions that set off the symptom. The Symptom-Context method (Luborsky, 1996) had its origins in such a generative moment.

EXAMPLE:
While I was listening to a patient on a spring day in 1963, she suddenly stopped talking and said, "Oh, I just forgot a thought. . . . What was it?" She paused. "Here it is." She had just recovered a memory about being rejected, a theme that seemed to fill her thoughts each time she experienced momentary forgetting.

Just as she recovered her thought, I had a serendipitous thought of my own: Why not use such defined moments in psychotherapy as material to study the conditions for the onset of both psychological and somatic symptoms? It was from experiences such as these that the Symptom-Context method grew.

That revelation dovetailed with an idea that had been with me for some years. I had treated a patient who had repeated reports of stomach pains during psychotherapy, and I began to catalogue them and to investigate their preconditions (Luborsky, 1953). Another strand of experience helped that process. I was doing collaborative research with my mentor, Raymond Cattell, that broke new ground on the sources and methods for psychotherapy research. During our research, we conducted the first longitudinal study using intraindividual factor analysis ("P-technique") of a patient in psychotherapy (Cattell & Luborsky, 1950; Luborsky, 1953, 1995). In other words, we were recurrently using as data the same patient over time, just as a therapist does. These clinical and research experiences gave rise to an investigation that led to the eventual development of the Symptom-Context method (Luborsky, 1996).

THE USES OF THE SYMPTOM-CONTEXT METHOD

The Symptom-Context method catches the symptom, along with its context, at the moment it appears. Looking for the triggers of symptoms is common clinical practice, but this approach focuses that practice on specific and immediate data. That focus is valuable, both as a clinical and a research method.

In clinical work, it gives a way for the patient and therapist to collaborate in their search for understanding. The emergence of the symptom is evident to both patient and therapist, and it can facilitate the patient's awareness of the links between a symptom and its meanings. This can be an illuminating experience for the patient, for whom the symptom may have previously been only a source of pain and frustration.

As a research method, it offers data on symptom formation that is usually only in the province of clinical hypotheses. Segments of a therapy session that surround a symptom—its *nodal points*—are compared with segments that do not surround a symptom—its *control nodal points*. These give rise to data on the symptom and its contextual conditions.

THEORIES OF SYMPTOM FORMATION

Symptoms look different through different lenses. To the patient, they are intrusions that are disturbing and sometimes painful. In the medical model, they are indications of a disorder or disease. In the past two decades, with the rise of knowledge in neurology and genetics, symptoms are more frequently seen in that light. Psychological explanations for symptom formation often put the feeling of helplessness at its core. Freud (1926/1959) saw the "neurotic symptom" as an attempted solution to a situation that was evaluated as so dangerous that the patient felt helpless and perhaps hopeless before it.

The Symptom-Context method does not preclude any form of explanation, since it is itself a lens on the symptom and its preconditions. However, it follows from an observation of Freud's that a main route to such understanding is through its "context." Freud stated that "the correct interpretation [of a symbol] can only be arrived at on each occasion from the context" (1900/1953, p. 353). The Symptom-Context method is based on this premise that the temporal sequence of each context may provide material that is thematically linked and so offers clues to its meaning.

CLINICAL APPLICATIONS OF THE SYMPTOM-CONTEXT METHOD

The Symptom-Context method is particularly helpful for patients with symptoms that they experience as mysterious or disturbing events. Patients with anxiety disorders, for example, can gain a sense of control by discovering the connection between their acute symptoms and other aspects of their lives. Demystifying the symptom can be a first step toward diminishing its power.

Symptoms of post-traumatic stress disorder are also well suited to this method because they may present clues about the original trauma. Physical symptoms that emerge during the session can become a vital part of the story as the patient connects them with their context.

EXAMPLE: Ms. Patricia Cutter Halifax

Ms. Halifax sought therapy due to frequent suicidal thoughts and a variety of medically unexplained bouts of constriction in the throat, making it abruptly difficult for her to speak.

P: "I knew he would be coming to Boston around now." Her voice is barely audible.

T: "You knew he would be coming near you, and now you can barely speak."

P: "Yeah. I hate it. It's like . . . [her voice gets even lower] like he's making me not talk." [She can barely squeeze out the words.]

They are talking about the patient's father, whom the patient now suspects abused her during childhood. She and the therapist are now "on the same page," finding that fears linked to her father affect her ability to breathe and then to speak.

While the Symptom-Context method's original purpose was to study the meanings of symptoms that occur within a session, it has been found to have clinical application for symptoms that occur outside of the session as well. This application can be initiated by listening for the immediate context for the onset of the symptom, as the patient tells of its occurrence. This application is illustrated through the treatment of a phobic patient who reported her outside-of-session symptoms and their contexts during the treatment (Luborsky, 1996).

Once patients are familiar with the method, they often look for links between the symptom and its context themselves, as illustrated by Ms. Turner:

EXAMPLE: Ms. Mary Turner

P: "I got the worst migraine this morning. I think it was because I was coming in here and what we have been talking about."

If there is a somatic component to the symptom, medical evaluation is recommended in order to rule out any medical condition. After that screening, the patient and therapist can search together to understand the psychological meanings of the symptom. Patients sometimes feel that such a shift means they are to blame for the symptom. Care should be taken to explore such concerns, which may present as an aspect of the patient's CCRT responses of self.

RESEARCH WITH THE SYMPTOM-CONTEXT METHOD

As a research method, the Symptom-Context method offers a means to compare repeated symptom-linked material with repeated non-symptom-linked material within the same patient. That is the basic definition of the Symptom-Context method in research, but alternative procedures may also be used. For example, the Symptom-Context sequence can be measured through either word units or time units.

By far the most ambitious and searching examination of patients with recurrent symptoms during psychotherapy sessions is presented in Luborsky (1996). The study included all of these symptoms: momentary forgetting, shifts in depression, phobias, stomach pains, cluster headaches, petit mal epileptic attacks, and premature ventricular contractions of the heart. This set of seven recurrent-symptom cases covered three mostly psychological and four mostly physical symptoms. These seven symptom cases are *all* of the cases that could be found that met the criteria even after an extensive worldwide, decade-long search (Luborsky, Stuart, et al., 2001). The criteria were that a transcript of the case must have been made and the presence of each recurrent symptom had to be noted at the exact point at which it emerged. Then, 12 qualities for each of the 50-word units *before* and 50-word units *after* each narrative in each recurrent-symptom case were assessed (see figure 5.1).

Recent research on the link between negative emotion and cardiac arrhythmia comes up with similar results, using a somewhat different method (Carels et al., 2003). In examining the link between a patient's negative moods and cardiac symptoms, the researchers asked 46 patients to keep diaries of mood states and symptoms. They found that cardiac symptoms were heightened with the buildup of negative emotion. These findings parallel the within-patient links between negative emotion and symptoms found with the Symptom-Context method.

The Symptom Emerges during the Buildup of a State of Helplessness

Across all seven different subjects with recurrent symptoms, the qualities of *hopelessness* and *lack of control* were the most pervasively connected. The analyses of each of the cases revealed the following order of each quality's effect sizes (i.e., the correlation of each measure with the combination). The list starts with the highest correlations and then descends in gradual order: (1) hopelessness, (2) lack of control, (3) anxiety, (4) blocked, (5) helplessness, (6) concern about supplies, (7) depression, (8) hostility to therapist, (9) guilt, (10) involvement with therapist, (11) separation concern, and (12) hostility to others.

EXAMPLE: Mr. Peter Berger

A vivid way to illustrate the psychological state that may lead to a symptom is to give examples of the Symptom-Context state just before a symptom develops in one patient over time, as in this example of a patient's recurrent headache. In that way, it becomes easier to see the conditions that build up before such symptoms.

Helplessness ending in hopelessness was the most prominent quality in all three of these examples. The therapist saw the buildup of the qualities before the headache and began to interpret to the patient the obvious presence of these qualities. However, in all three samples given here with their verbatim contexts, the headache, once initiated, continued to develop. That is probably because the headache was already launched as a physical event, but it could also be due to the feeling state of the context, which continued during the session.

The 50-word samples of patient's words came prior to each cluster headache (from Luborsky, 1996, p. 388ff).

Sample 1 in Session 104: The 50-Word Sample Just before a Headache

P: I can't say it is, uh [pause], unbearable. I mean, it's bearable. It's just not too pleasant. [Pause of 2 min] I always had some thoughts of going down South for a while and working in one of the registration drives. Frankly, one of the things that stopped me was coming here [to the treatment sessions] twice a week. [Pause]

T: Going down there and working on the registration would give you more of a feeling of—

P: [Interrupting] Involvement.

T: Involvement.

P: Of some meaning.

T: Yeah, would fill you up more.

P: Mmm-hmm.

T: Coming here prevents you from being filled up, from that point of view.

P: Yeah, yeah.

T: Prevents you from doing something that would fill you up more, hmm?

P: Yeah. Of course, my work would prevent my, you know, my—any prolonged stay, too. Well, but I mean, that was the thought that made me dismiss it, I realized that I would be coming here. [Pause of 3 ? min] I'm starting to get a little minor headache.

[He shows the appearance of developing a serious *headache*.]

Sample 2 in Session 107: Another 50-Word Sample Just before a Headache

T: It's funny; a little while ago you were saying it's funny that everything you say pointed to your feeling in a bind, but you don't feel in a bind. And right now you're saying, "I do feel in a bind."

P: Yes, right now I do, yeah. [Long pause] And now I'm not even thinking clearly. [Long pause]

T: You said that a part of the bind is that you want to go on and talk about a different subject.

P: Mmm-hmm.

T: The idea must be that somewhere you feel that I am binding you, like the guy in the dream, to talk about certain subjects. You want to go off and talk about some *other* subjects.

P: Well, that, and the fact that I think the other subject's so dried out; I have nothing to say about it, you know. Uh, I don't know what, uh, how to, uh, respond, uh.

T: Hmmm.

P: [Long pause of 20 s] This, you know, this never happened anyplace else but here. I usually don't get in the, into the . . . in the, in these binds. [Pause of 10 s]

T: You didn't get into a bind about registration?

P: Well, not to the extent that I'm tongue-tied. You know, I can't think.

T: You were in a bind with the Alka-Seltzer, in a bind in relation to the bar, or in a bind in any other area?

P: No, I mean now I'm just tongue-tied, can't even think straight.

T: In a bind in your dream?

P: Well, in the dream, yeah. No, I mean, I . . . I, I'm not forced to lapse into these total silences and uhh, you know. [Long pause of 50 s] Now, I think I'm starting to get a headache. Uh . . .

[He shows the appearance of developing a *headache*.]

Sample 3 in Session 128: Another 50-Word Sample before a Headache

T: But you still feel maybe I'm still dissatisfied with you, though, about how you've been able to do.

P: Yeah, yeah. You're becoming a dissatisfied mother again—

T: [Laughs]

P: [Continues] Uh, Z's [a pet name the patient made up as a term for himself at that moment] not coming through. But the feeling has that quality. I'm not uneasy. I just thought that I would put it on the table, you know.

T: OK, Z, you did put it on the table.

P: Yeah. Um, I don't know; maybe I just don't understand what I should do in these sessions as much as I think I understand. I think by this time, I know. But maybe I am. . . . [Pause]

T: I think you do understand. But I think you—what I sense, mainly, is that you're wondering whether I'm satisfied with your ability to go back over it. OK? Whether I'm still mad at you.

P: Not so much my ability—my willingness. Maybe I'm taking it for granted that you think I am able to do it. Um, but I still sense that you think I am unwilling to do it. And I don't think I am. Maybe I'm fooling myself. But I don't think I am. And I think that I'm trying, too.

T: Yes, you are. I know you are.

P: I, I, I, when I go out, I assess the meetings. When I leave here, I'm usually getting a mild headache. [The patient began to look as if he was starting to get a headache.]

T: Are you getting one now?

P: Yeah, just a mild one. It's not going to be anything. [He typically very much underestimated his headaches when they occurred during a session.]

The Psychological State before a Headache in Other Sessions with Mr. Peter Berger

During other sessions as well in which a headache was reported, the patient's involvement with the therapist revealed the building of another acute state of lack of control and a feeling of not getting the response he desperately needed.

The first time the patient developed a headache during a session (Session 73), he had looked forward to talking about a book with the therapist and began the session by speaking about the book for 5 or 10 minutes. But as soon as the therapist stopped talking about the book and began to refer to the patient's feelings in telling the account, the patient's headache started. When the explicit discussion about the book resumed a few minutes later, his headache disappeared. Because of the on-off sequence of the appearance then disappearance of the headache, it had the quality of a controlled experiment!

The patient explained the ins and outs of the headache's appearance in terms of lack of control and consequent hopelessness: When the therapist put aside talking about the book, Mr. Berger felt he had no power to ask the therapist to resume the discussion. If the therapist wanted to change the subject, the patient felt he could do nothing about it. When the therapist asked him what had pleased him in speaking about the book, the patient replied that he wanted a particular kind of closeness with the therapist—the feeling of two men, two professionals, talking about something they know in common.

Another headache developed in Session 92. Just before the headache started, the patient began to say what he keenly felt: He was dull and would not be able to get a positive response from the therapist because the patient himself knew that what he, the patient, had presented was dull. At that point, a headache began. At no point did the patient fully question his powerlessness to affect the therapist's inclination about the topic the therapist would talk about.

The headaches occuring outside the session seemed, from his accounts (as rated by the therapist), to have had similar contexts to those occuring in the session, with two important differences: (1) The relationship with the therapist was less explicit for headaches outside the session, and (2) the amount of obvious anger and even rage was far greater *outside* the session. Therefore, it seems likely that the patient had been suppressing or avoiding direct expressions of anger when headaches developed in the therapist's presence. He said, for example, in Session 130, "I know when I have headaches, the more anger the worse the headache."

Following are the findings of the Symptom-Context method, when applied to this case, that reflect these principles:

Principle 1: The Context Preceding a Symptom Differs from the Context Preceding a Nonsymptom

Finding: The conditions in the immediate context of the headache patient's words significantly differentiated the headache segments from the control segments.

The differentiation in this case was *within* ratings of the 50-word units before the headache: (in order, starting with the highest first) blocked, lack of control, hopelessness, dependent, helplessness, hostility to therapist, anxiety, and doubt.

Principle 2: The Background State May Show Some of the Same Qualities

Finding: For the conditions in the larger background state, some of the same qualities as in the Symptom-Context were evident in terms of the feeling of lessened control.

These also were shown in terms of the long pauses, stuttering, negative affect, and score on a scoring system called "the helplessness manual."

Principle 3: The Background State and the Immediate Context Interact

Finding: Two classes of conditions appeared to interact in contributing to the migraine-like headaches in this patient.

The immediate context conditions and the broad background conditions reinforced each other, producing heightened negative affect and feelings of lack of control around the onset of symptoms.

SUMMARY AND DISCUSSION

This chapter describes the clinical and research applications of the Symptom-Context method. It explains how examination of the immediate context for a symptom that emerges during a psychotherapy session aids in understanding the symptom.

The use of this method to understand a recurrent symptom has been illustrated through the example of the frequent headaches of Mr. Peter Berger. We found significantly different qualities that distinguished the preheadache segments from the precontrol (nonsymptom) segments. The prominent qualities were all those of negative emotion and lack of control: blocked, lack of control, hopelessness, dependent, helplessness, hostility toward the therapist, anxiety, and doubt. We also examined the larger background state outside of the relationship episodes and found some similar although less intense states of helplessness and lack of control, some of which were evident in behavior. We have shown that *both types of immediate context conditions and the broad background context conditions interact in helping to set off the migraine-like headaches of this patient.*

In conclusion, the Symptom-Context method offers a way to understand the meaning of a symptom as it appears in an evident context, from the start to the emergence of the symptom. It has been found to be clinically applicable

		Symptom Begins			Symptom Ends	
Symptom-Context	50 words	W, RO, RS 1a	0	0	W, RO, RS 1b	50 words
Control 1 (Other parts of same session)	50 words	W, RO, RS 1c	0	0	W, RO, RS 1d	50 words
Control 2 (Other sessions)	50 words	W, RO, RS 1e	0	0	W, RO, RS 1f	50 words

Figure 5.1. The Symptom-Context method

to stress-related medical conditions, as well as to anxiety disorders and post-traumatic stress disorder.

The Symptom-Context method has shown promise for finding the psychological meaning of recurrent symptoms and behaviors (Luborsky, 1996). More study of the links of certain emotional states to the onset of stress-linked medical problems is needed. The method has considerable potential for further clinical and research discoveries.

Chapter Six

The Health-Sickness Rating Scale (HSRS) Method

Our research on this particular topic began at the Menninger Foundation around 1949, at a time when there was no standardized way to determine a patient's mental health. We observed that case histories written by a clinician tended to include an initial evaluation of the degree of health versus sickness of the patient. Our aim was to develop a reliable and valid measure to quantify that process. It was one of the earliest research transformations of a clinical concept, and it became known as the Health-Sickness Rating Scale (HSRS) (Luborsky, 1962). We guessed—and we were right—that it would also turn out to be a predictive factor for the outcome of psychotherapy (Luborsky, Diguer, et al., 1993).

The Health-Sickness Rating Scale offers a global rating, so the severity of a patient's condition can be assessed for both clinical and quantitative research purposes. Since research regularly links initial psychological health with treatment outcome, it is helpful to have ways to partial out its effects in comparative treatment studies.

In SE psychotherapy, assessing the Health-Sickness level of a patient helps the therapist determine the appropriate mix of supportive and expressive elements. Since patients with more serious levels of disturbance tend to need more support, the early assessment of Health-Sickness level can be a useful guide for the therapist. The scale itself is given here (see figure 6.1), as well as in Luborsky (1962). As can be seen, the scale has a central line extending from 0 to 100, with 100 being a rosy state of mental health. Examples of nodal levels are given in words on the accompanying scale, with numerical equivalents alongside them.

Definition of Scale Points		Examples of Scale Points
100 An ideal state of complete functioning integration, resiliency in the face of stress, happiness and social effectiveness.	100	Some patients who complete treatment will fall within this category, as well as some patients who come for and need only "situational" counseling.
(99 to 76: Degrees of "everyday" adjustment problems. Few of these people seek Rx.)		
75 At 75, inhibitions, symptoms, character problems become severe enough to cause more than "everyday" discomfort. Some of these people seek Rx.	75	Very mild neuroses or addictions and behavior disorders begin here and can be scored further down depending on severity.
65 At 65 generally functioning pretty well but has *focalized* problem or more *generalized* lack of effectiveness without specific symptoms.	65	Most phobias and other clearly neurotic conditions.
50 At 50 definitely needs Rx to continue to work satisfactorily and shows increasing difficulty maintaining self autonomously (even without expressed or recognized need for formal Rx). Patient may either be in a stable unsatisfactory adjustment (where most energy is bound in the conflicts) or in an unstable adjustment from which he or she will very likely regress.	50	Severe neuroses, such as severe obsessive-compulsiveness, may be rated at 50 on down. Some *compensated* psychoses.
	35	Most borderline schizophrenics; psychotic depressives; patients with severe character problems.
25 At 25, obviously unable to function autonomously. Needs hospital protection (or would need it if it were not for the support of the therapist). (The fact that the patient is in the hospital doesn't mean he *must* be rated at this point—he may have changed since admission or be in for other reasons.)	25	Most clear-cut, overt psychoses; psychotic characters; more severe addictions (that require hospital care).
10 At 10, extremely difficult to make any contact with patient. Needs closed-ward care. Not much chance of continued existence without care.	10	Clearly psychotic patients.
(24 to 1: Increased loss of contact with reality; the degree of regression requires a need for protection of patient or others from the patient.)		
0 Any condition which if unattended would quickly result in the patient's death, but not necessarily by his own hand.	0	Completely regressed schizophrenics; patients who are incontinent, out of contact, or require complete nursing care and tube feedings; patients in the terminal state of Huntington's chorea; patients with status epilepticus.

Figure 6.1. The numerical equivalents of the gradations of severity of the Health-Sickness Rating Scale.

THE ORIGINS OF THE HSRS

The HSRS method was designed as a way to get a basic measure of a patient's level of mental health. It has been applied to data from psychotherapy sessions, as well as to the assessment of the current state of the patient (Luborsky, 1962). The first paper on the HSRS was based on data collected with the help of my research group (Luborsky, 1962). The HSRS research group at the Menninger Foundation included Benjamin Rubenstein (chairman), Gerald Aronson, Paul Bergman, Michalina Fabian, Robert R. Holt, Helmut Kaiser, Gardner Murphy, Donald Watterson, and Lester Luborsky. A second and more general paper as a further check on its reliability was prepared with Henry Bachrach (Luborsky & Bachrach, 1974). A third paper by Armelius, Gerin, and Luborsky (1985) showed that the HSRS was an even more discriminating measure than those used in other parts of the world. The HSRS has been translated into many languages, including Swedish, French, Hebrew, Italian, and Russian.

The HSRS was slightly revised to become the Global Assessment of Functioning (Endicott, Spitzer, Fleiss, & Cohen, 1976). That scale was then revised to become Axis V in the *Diagnostic and Statistical Manual* (*DSM*). In this form, it is part of the usual diagnostic repertoire in the assessment of patients.

The adequate attribution of the HSRS was first footnoted in *DSM-IV* (*American Psychiatric Association Diagnostic and Statistical Manual of Mental Disorders*, 4th ed., 1994, p. 32). This occurred only after my protesting through letters and phone calls to the Diagnostic and Statistical Manual Committee of the American Psychiatric Association, eventually gaining the support of Robert Spitzer. The committee ultimately agreed to visibly reference my original (1962) paper as the correct source for their Global Assessment of Functioning (GAF) scale.

USES OF THE HSRS

1. *To improve estimates of mental health.* The HSRS gives a functional estimate of mental health. While we recognized quite early that an evaluation of Health-Sickness of any patient was needed to better plan the treatment, we later found that the presence and carrying out of such planning was also one of the predictive factors in determining the outcome of psychotherapy.

   The HSRS method started with our finding that Health-Sickness could be presented in numbers, even more precisely than in words alone. We therefore decided to use *both* words and numbers. It also turned out that the quantification aided in establishing degrees of HSRS as a useful unit for clinical research.
2. *To adapt the HSRS to different groups.* The HSRS continues to be widely used. A variety of applications have been made with the HSRS, including *an adaptation for children* by Paulina Kernberg (Liebowitz, Rembar, Kernberg, Frankel, & Kruger, 1988).

3. *To predict psychotherapy outcome*. The relation between HSRS measures and estimations of the outcomes of treatment has been consistently noted. A long series of studies have offered good evidence of the predicted relation of psychological health with the outcome of treatment (Luborsky, Diguer, et al., 1993; McLellan, Luborsky, Woody, O'Brien, & Druley, 1983). In other words, in terms of the "riches" of treatment in the form of psychological health, "the rich get richer."
4. *To order the severity of the cases in a collection*. The existence of the HSRS played a big part in the gradual assembly of the Penn Psychoanalytic Treatment Collection (Luborsky, Stuart, et al., 2001)—the first such collection to be found anywhere. This collection of 17 cases is the only set of complete and recorded psychoanalyses that are available as a research resource. In research with this data set, Health-Sickness turned out to be a moderately successful predictive factor: A correlation was reported in this paper of .60 between HSRS and outcome.

SUMMARY AND DISCUSSION

The HSRS was the first scale to offer a method to reliably establish the level of psychological health, both in words and in numbers. An adaptation of the scale now serves as Axis V in the *Diagnostic and Statistical Manual of Mental Disorders*. The HSRS can be used for the purposes of both clinical and research work. In clinical work, the SE psychotherapist can estimate the proportion of supportive versus expressive elements in the treatment, based on the mental health of the patient. In clinical research, the role of the Health-Sickness level of a patient or patient group can be reliably estimated in relation to outcome. It has been found to be a central contributing factor in psychotherapy research.

Chapter Seven

The Helping-Alliance (HA) Methods

Since helping is at the crux of psychotherapy, the Helping Alliance is fundamental to the process. Here are brief examples of two kinds of Helping Alliance at work:

EXAMPLE: Ms. Deborah Kaplan

P: "I was glad we had an appointment scheduled today. It's been a long week."

EXAMPLE: Mr. Rob Harper

P: "So I told him I could do it. I have no idea how I'll get the guts to do a job like that, but I just thought we'd figure it out somehow."

Both of these patients are expressing faith in the Helping Alliance they have formed with their therapists to carry them through. The first patient seems to be anticipating that the therapist will help her feel better (Helping Alliance, type 1), while the second patient alludes to *working together* with the therapist to overcome a problem (Helping Alliance, type 2).

The Helping Alliance is a term for the degree to which the patient experiences the relationship with the therapist as helpful or potentially helpful in achieving the patient's goals in psychotherapy (Luborsky, 1976, 1977, 2000a). Other similar terms probably refer to the same phenomenon; early examples include the "therapeutic alliance" (Zetzel, 1958) and the "working alliance" (Greenson, 1967). Greenson describes the working alliance as a *reality-based collaboration* between patient and therapist, thus distinguishing it from the transference.

According to Horvath, Gaston, and Luborsky (1993), "There is empirical corroboration of Freud's original proposition that a friendly, sympathetic attitude toward the client is beneficial in the initial development of the alliance"

(p. 204). Early alliance measures are significantly correlated with measures of the therapist's empathy, as well as with the outcomes of psychotherapy. It could be the "sleeper variable" underneath other techniques. However, in order to examine the role of the alliance in psychotherapy, there needs to be a way to measure it. The Helping Alliance methods offer the first instruments to measure this aspect of the therapeutic relationship so that its potential contribution to the process and outcome of psychotherapy can be investigated by clinical research. It was in 1976 and 1977 that I began to try measures of the Helping Alliance. Since that time, a variety of methods have been used as alliance measures: Barber, Connolly, Crits-Christoph, Gladis, and Siqueland (2000); Gaston, Thompson, Gallagher, Cournoyer, and Gagnon (1998); and Piper, Azim, Joyce, and McCallum (1991).

While the importance of an alliance between the patient and therapist is implicit in all clinical work, the Helping Alliance measures provide ways to make its role explicit by quantifying the definition of the concept. Well over 100 research studies have been published on the Helping Alliance during the past two decades (Horvath, Gaston, & Luborsky, 1993). Its relationship to treatment outcome has been consistently positive, and the degree of correlation is moderately high. We found Pearson correlations of .65 and higher between the Helping Alliance and behavioral measures, such as drug use, employment, and other similar behaviors (Luborsky, McLellan, Woody, O'Brien, & Auerbach, 1985). In short, having a way to quantify the therapeutic alliance has gone a long way toward assessing its value.

Again, the Helping Alliance measure has two subtypes, conveniently called Helping Alliance, type 1, and Helping Alliance, type 2 (Luborsky, 2000a). Type 1 refers to a Helping Alliance in which the patient experiences the therapist as providing the help. Type 2 refers to an alliance between the therapist and patient in which they are working together in a team effort to help the patient. The two subtypes of the Helping Alliance are highly correlated with each other, and both are independently correlated with good treatment outcome.

These robust results are clinically useful. They tell us that the relational aspects of treatment are linked to its outcome. It matters that the patient experiences the therapist as "there for him," as in the Helping Alliance, Type 1, and that the patient feels the two of them have formed a working partnership aimed at solving the patient's problems (Type 2). Taken together, a positive Helping Alliance is one of the factors that has been found to underlie success in treatment.

RESEARCH ON THE HELP OF THE HELPING ALLIANCE

Studies of the Helping Alliance suggest it plays an important role in treatment of different diagnoses. The HAq-II method has been applied to the study of treatment with *adjustment disorders* (Strain, Newcorn, Wolf, & Fulop, 1994). The study shows the power of high Helping Alliance as a predictor of treatment outcome in adjustment disorders.

The role of the Helping Alliance in the treatment of both *major and minor depression* has also been studied. Selmi, Klein, Greist, and Sorrell (1990) found that a high Helping Alliance was associated with high improvement in both forms of depression, as compared with a control condition.

These results suggest that the Helping Alliance plays an important role in the treatment of varied diagnoses. That makes it an important variable to continue to study. It could be that a positive Helping Alliance contributes to hope, a quality that is probably pivotal in any form of treatment.

MEASURING THE HELPING ALLIANCE

The Helping Alliance can be measured in three ways. The first is the "counting signs" method (HAcs), which refers to finding specific signs in the patient's statements that disclose an alliance. The second method is the "global rating" method (HAr), in which a section of the session is rated for its alliance qualities. In the third method, a section of the transcript is developed as a *questionnaire* (HAq) to be answered by the patient and by the therapist. (See tables 7.1 through 7.3.)

HAcs VERSUS HAr

The "counting signs" and the "global rating" methods both have particular assets. The first method, the HAcs, contributes to the validity of working with the details of the transcript. However, it does require the effort to make a transcript and then to search for each example of the subtype. The HAr refers to the global rating of a whole segment; it has the advantage of greater simplicity because the session can be remembered or replayed from a tape recording and given a single set of ratings of each subtype. Although at first glance the HAcs, which relies on the details of the verbatim material, would seem the more reliable, the two methods are highly intercorrelated. We found a correlation of .83 for positive HAcs with HAr, which implies that the judges could base their ratings on expressions of the Helping Alliance as described in the HAcs manual (Luborsky, Crits-Christoph, Alexander, Margolis, & Cohen, 1983; Alexander & Luborsky, 1986).

The first method, HAcs, contains these four subtypes of type 1: (1) the patient believes the therapist or therapy is helping, (2) the patient feels changed since the beginning of the treatment, (3) the patient feels understood by the

Table 7.1. Helping Alliance Methods

	Measurements	*Researchers and Date*	*Source*	*Method*
HAcs	HAcs: counting signs (type 1)	Luborsky, 1976, 1977	Rating of signs in a session	Ratings
HAr	HAr: observer's global rating of sessions (type 2)	Luborsky, 1976, 1977	Rating of signs in a session	Observer's global rating
HAq	HAq-I: 11-item questionnaire	Luborsky, Crits-Christoph, Mintz, & Auerbach, 1988	Rating by self and by therapist	Questionnaire with ratings of each item
	HAq-II: 19-item questionnaire	Luborsky, 1994; Luborsky, Barber, et al., 1996	Rating by self and by therapist	Questionnaire with ratings of each item

Table 7.2. The Helping Alliance Questionnaire–II (Patient Version)

INSTRUCTIONS: These are ways that a person may feel or behave in relation to another person—the therapist. Consider carefully your relationship with your therapist, and then mark each statement according to how strongly you agree or disagree. Please mark every one.

	Strongly Disagree	*Disagree*	*Slightly Disagree*	*Slightly Agree*	*Agree*	*Strongly Agree*
1. I feel I can depend upon the therapist.	1	2	3	4	5	6
2. I feel the therapist understands me.	1	2	3	4	5	6
3. I feel the therapist wants me to	1	2	3	4	5	6
achieve my goals.	1	2	3	4	5	6
4. At times I distrust the therapist's judgment.						
5. I feel I am working together with the therapist in a joint effort.	1	2	3	4	5	6
6. I believe we have similar ideas about the nature of my problems.	1	2	3	4	5	6
7. I generally respect the therapist's views about me.	1	2	3	4	5	6
8. The procedures used in my therapy are not well suited to my needs.	1	2	3	4	5	6
9. I like the therapist as a person.	1	2	3	4	5	6
10. In most sessions, the therapist and I find a way to work on my problems together.	1	2	3	4	5	6
11. The therapist relates to me in ways that slow down the progress of the therapy.	1	2	3	4	5	6
12. A good relationship has formed with my therapist.	1	2	3	4	5	6

Continued

Table 7.2. *(Continued)*

	Strongly Disagree	*Disagree*	*Slightly Disagree*	*Slightly Agree*	*Agree*	*Strongly Agree*
13. The therapist appears to be experienced in helping people.	1	2	3	4	5	6
14. I want very much to work out my problems.	1	2	3	4	5	6
15. The therapist and I have meaningful exchanges.	1	2	3	4	5	6
16. The therapist and I sometimes have unprofitable exchanges.	1	2	3	4	5	6
17. From time to time, we both talk about the same important events in my past.	1	2	3	4	5	6
18. I believe the therapist likes me as a person.	1	2	3	4	5	6
19. At times the therapist seems distant.	1	2	3	4	5	6

Table 7.3. The Helping Alliance Questionnaire–II (Therapist Version)

INSTRUCTIONS: These are ways that a person may feel or behave in relation to another person—the patient. Consider carefully your relationship with your patient, and then mark each statement according to how strongly you agree or disagree. Please mark every one.

	Strongly Disagree	*Disagree*	*Slightly Disagree*	*Slightly Agree*	*Agree*	*Strongly Agree*
1. The patient feels he/she can depend upon me.	1	2	3	4	5	6
2. He/she feels I understand him/her.	1	2	3	4	5	6
3. The patient feels I want him/her to achieve the goals.	1	2	3	4	5	6
4. At times the patient distrusts my judgment.	1	2	3	4	5	6

Table 7.3. ***(Continued)***

	Strongly Disagree	*Disagree*	*Slightly Disagree*	*Slightly Agree*	*Agree*	*Strongly Agree*
5. The patient feels he/she is working together with me in a joint effort.	1	2	3	4	5	6
6. I believe we have similar ideas about the nature of his/her problems.	1	2	3	4	5	6
7. The patient generally respects my views about him/her.	1	2	3	4	5	6
8. The patient believes the procedures used in his/her therapy are not well suited to his/her needs.	1	2	3	4	5	6
9. The patient likes me as a person.	1	2	3	4	5	6
10. In most sessions, we find a way to work on his/her problems together.	1	2	3	4	5	6
11. The patient believes I relate to him/her in ways that slow down the progress of the therapy.	1	2	3	4	5	6
12. The patient believes a good relationship has formed between us.	1	2	3	4	5	6
13. The patient believes I am experienced in helping people.	1	2	3	4	5	6
14. I want very much for the patient to work out his/her problems.	1	2	3	4	5	6

Continued

Table 7.3. *(Continued)*

	Strongly Disagree	*Disagree*	*Slightly Disagree*	*Slightly Agree*	*Agree*	*Strongly Agree*
15. The patient and I have meaningful exchanges.	1	2	3	4	5	6
16. The patient and I sometimes have unprofitable exchanges.	1	2	3	4	5	6
17. From time to time, we both talk about the same important events in his/her past.	1	2	3	4	5	6
18. The patient believes I like him/her as a person.	1	2	3	4	5	6
19. At times the patient sees me as distant.	1	2	3	4	5	6

therapist, and (4) the patient feels optimistic and confident that the therapist and the treatment can help. The three type-2 subtypes include the following: (1) the patient experiences working together with the therapist in a team effort, (2) the patient shares with the therapist similar conceptions about the bases of the problems, and (3) the patient demonstrates similar qualities to those of the therapist, especially those connected with ability to use the therapist's tools for understanding.

An interesting result came from the HAcs method on the predictive value of positive versus negative Helping Alliance signs (Constantino, Castonguay, & Schut, 2002). Early positive Helping Alliance signs were found to be significant predictors of the outcome of the treatment, while the negative signs were poor predictors. This finding of the predictive value of the early positive Helping Alliance signs supports the view of those who believe in the role of early positive relationships in psychotherapy. Also, this principle suggests that negative Helping Alliance signs do not necessarily mean the treatment is likely to have a poor outcome; rather, the therapist should concentrate therapeutic work on the negative signs because they may be indications of the patient's relationship problems. This appears to fit with Freud's principle of technique, which recommends going along with the positive transference while interpreting the negative transference statements (Freud, 1912a/1958; Luborsky, 2000a).

THE USES OF THE HELPING ALLIANCE QUESTIONNAIRE: FORM II

The third method was developed in the form of questionnaires, Helping Alliance Form I and Helping Alliance Form II (Luborsky, 2000a). The second form is an enlarged version of the first—the kind of self-report item originally started by Barrett-Lennard (1962) and now described in the Helping Alliance Questionnaire–II (Luborsky, Barber, et al., 1996).

Because the Form II questionnaire is an enlarged, improved version of Form I, most of the explanation and recommendations that follow concern Form II (Luborsky, Barber, et al., 1996). The Helping Alliance Questionnaire II is therefore the best way to predict the outcomes of psychotherapy; briefly described by Luborsky (1994) and Luborsky, Diguer, Kaechele, et al. (1999), it is used as a self-rating and a rating of the other person in the narrative. This 19-item HAq-II is the main form now used. It can prove to be clinically helpful in detecting and evaluating a period of low alliance. Such periods need clinical attention, either through amplifying the supportive relationship, as discussed in chapter 9, or by applying the techniques of *rupture and repair* (Safran, Muran, Samstag, & Stevens, 2001), where the therapist examines—with the patient—what has gone wrong in the therapy and makes an effort to acknowledge the rupture problem and to repair it.

OTHER MEASURES OF THE ALLIANCE

Since the development of the Helping Alliance measures, many other predictive measures have been developed. Here are five of them, including those for the Helping Alliance, all of which tend to intercorrelate significantly (Tichenor & Hill, 1989): (1) California Psychotherapy Alliance Scales, CALPAS (Gaston, 1991), and CALTRAS (Marmar, Weiss, & Gaston, 1989); (2) Penn Helping Alliance Scales, Penn HAcs, HAr, and HAq (Alexander & Luborsky, 1986; Luborsky, Crits-Christoph, et al., 1983); (3) Therapeutic Alliance Scales, TAS (Marziali, 1984); (4) Vanderbilt Therapeutic Alliance Scale, VTAS, and Vanderbilt Psychotherapy Process Scale, VPPS (O'Malley, Suh, & Strupp, 1983); and (5) Working Alliance Inventory, WAI (Horvath, 1982).

SUMMARY AND DISCUSSION

The creation of a positive Helping Alliance predicts good outcome in psychotherapy. In order to understand more about its role, it needs to be measured effectively. The Helping Alliance measures allow its role to be better understood.

The HAcs, the HAr, and the HAq-I (11 items) (see appendix B), which was revised and enlarged as the HAq-II (19 items) (Luborsky, 2000a), offer ways to study the alliance. The HAq-II has been shown to have moderately high to high intercorrelations with the Penn Helping Alliance measures and other related alliance measures (Tichenor & Hill, 1989; Tang & DeRubeis, 1999). It has a relatively high predictive value, as reported here. The high intercorrelation between the different methods of studying the Helping Alliance tell something of its power. Counting specific signs, using clinical judgment to listen for the quality of an alliance, and recording responses to the Helping Alliance questionnaire are all able to pick up the quality of the Helping Alliance.

PART III

DOING SUPPORTIVE-EXPRESSIVE (SE) PSYCHOTHERAPY

Chapter Eight

The Opening Phase of SE Psychotherapy

In the beginning of psychotherapy, everything is new. No matter what else the patient may have done to try to solve his problems or how many times he might have been in treatment before, this encounter is a first. It brings with it the patient's hopes, along with his fears and his problems. The therapist's first job is to attune herself to this new person and listen to what he brings. This simple act is actually complex since it involves listening at several different levels at once. Some patients begin their treatment with clear goals; others come with problems that cause distress but are hard to put into words. In either case, the therapist needs to keep an open ear to different aspects of the patient's problems and ways of being.

The therapist begins with an opening statement such as "What brings you here?" or any equivalent question about problems in the patient's life that prompted him to seek treatment. The therapist listens for these three dimensions in the patient's response:

1. *The direct answer*. What does the patient see as the chief problem?
2. *The background sequence*. What has led up to the problem?
3. *The current context*. What is the current context for the problem?

The therapist also attends to the patient's ways of relating and the following emotional dimensions:

1. *The relational framework*. How does the patient relate to the therapist?
2. *The emotional tone*. How actively distressed does the patient appear? What kind of affect state is there?
3. *The level of stability*. How stable is the patient? How well is he functioning in his life?

In order to take in all these levels of information, the therapist needs to be, or to become, adept at attending to the patient's communications. This involves *open listening* to the varied levels of communication while staying focused on the immediate data. The different forms of listening are explored further in chapter 10.

The early sessions are typically a time to gather information, as well as to set the frame and goals of the treatment. If the patient does not spontaneously offer the basic facts of his life situation and reasons for treatment, the therapist may want to pose some questions.

The therapist needs to convey a focused interest in the patient and his problems. She also must attend to the verbal and nonverbal ways the patient expresses himself, as well as to the content the patient conveys. Meanwhile, the patient will be gathering a sense of the therapist and the "enterprise" of psychotherapy. He will bring both his ways of perceiving and his experiences with important others, perhaps including other therapists.

The therapist's initial efforts are aimed at being receptive to this new patient and hearing the problems and themes he conveys. In that way the therapist begins the tasks of establishing a Helping Alliance and gathering information about the patient's Core Conflictual Relationship Theme (CCRT).

EXAMPLE: Ms. June Samuelson

Ms. Samuelson is smiling as she sits down in the chair, but her pinched expression doesn't match her smile.

P: [With the remnants of a smile] It's not that bad.

T: [The therapist waits.]

P: I have things to be grateful for. Probably a lot of people who come in here have terrible lives, bad things going on, and I can't say that.

T: [The therapist nods.]

P: I guess you are wondering *why* I came in here. . . .

T: I *am* interested in hearing about that.

So far Ms. Samuelson has yet to give her "chief complaint," but the therapist has been engaged in two things at the same time. She is listening to what the patient is saying and to what the patient is not saying in words.

As her opening move, the patient is doing more *conveying* than *saying*. This is beginning information for the therapist about this patient's CCRT: She appears to feel as if she should diminish her own needs while comparing them to the greater needs of imagined others. This may be linked to a heightened concern about others' reactions. But it is much too soon for the therapist to be sure about those potential themes or hypotheses. Instead, the therapist conveys an interest in what the patient brings—and a readiness to listen. In that way the therapist is directing her first moves toward the beginning of a Helping Alliance while listening for the unfolding of the patient's personal themes.

FRAMING THE TREATMENT

After the initial one to three sessions, the therapist will summarize essential aspects of the treatment the patient is beginning (Grenyer, 2002), including the following:

1. Restating or clarifying the patient's main goals
2. Discussing the frequency and length of the sessions
3. Determining the fee
4. Describing any policies the therapist may have about missed or cancelled appointments
5. Giving some sense of the anticipated length of treatment (in a time-limited treatment, that will be the number of sessions planned; in an open-ended treatment it might be "until we see clear signs of improvement" or "we will review your therapy again as we get to know your problems better")

INITIAL UNDERSTANDING

The therapist also needs to convey an initial understanding of the patient's problems before the close of the opening phase (i.e., a beginning understanding of what the patient has said so far). The therapist's empathy for the patient and her problems should be conveyed within that segment. This offers to the patient a beginning sense that she was heard, along with a sense that the therapist is someone who may be able to help.

If the patient expresses discouragement about the prospect of treatment, that theme should be heard as an opportunity to understand the patient's feelings and prior experiences. If the patient describes being frequently disappointed by people, the possibility of those feelings emerging in therapy may also be mentioned at this point. In these ways, the therapist is letting the patient know that such feelings can be discussed rather than simply acted upon.

It is sometimes true that early problems mean a problematic match between patient and therapist. In that case, the therapist can facilitate a change. However, often such doubts are early indications of problems with trust or hope that will need to be welcomed into the treatment, problems that will become an important aspect of CCRT work.

SUMMARY AND DISCUSSION

The opening phase of treatment combines different forms of information processing. The therapist begins a process of empathic listening while also gathering initial impressions of the patient's relationships that will develop toward an exploration of the patient's core themes. These aspects of the opening phase continue into the next phases of treatment. The therapist also collects specific information and sets the frame for the treatment. Here is a summary of the therapist's central tasks during the opening phase of psychotherapy:

1. *Listen* for the patient's treatment goals, either directly or indirectly expressed.
2. *Explain* and demonstrate how the therapy will proceed.
3. *Make arrangements* for the structure of the treatment.
4. *Respond with* an attitude of interest, acceptance, and empathy for the patient's affect state.
5. *Encourage* a partnership with the patient by inviting open expression.
6. *Gather information* about relationships that will allow the CCRT to be formulated.

Chapter Nine

The Supportive Relationship: Its Hows and Whys

"Support" in psychotherapy has typically been viewed as a necessary but secondary aspect of treatment, not needing too much planning—rather like packing a pair of shoes in preparation for a journey. Yet clinical research findings rate the Helping Alliance, and the sense of support that it brings, as one of the few factors consistently linked with a good treatment outcome. Two empirical studies show that greater support by the therapist is related to better outcome (Morgan, Luborsky, Crits-Christoph, Curtis, & Solomon, 1982; Buckley, Conte, Plutchik, Wild, & Karasu, 1984). Putting both of these studies together yields a mean correlation of .61, a fairly adequate correlation for clinical research. Similarly, the presence of support was highly ranked in the summary of all studies by Orlinsky, Grawe, and Parks (1994). These robust findings suggest that the role of support in psychotherapy deserves more attention.

A supportive relationship is one in which the patient feels bolstered by the therapist and by the treatment. Prominent among the components of supportiveness are a positive Helping Alliance, the therapist's empathy, and the structure of the treatment itself. The therapist's empathy for the patient's emotional states deepens the experience of support, while the therapist's explicit statements of support can strengthen it. The structure of the treatment builds a reliable expectation of help into the patient's life so that the structure itself becomes a support. With some patients, the therapist's interest in the real elements of their lives bolsters the support given by the treatment (as in Bond, Banon, & Grenier, 1998).

PRINCIPLE 1: ALL PSYCHOTHERAPIES GIVE SOME SUPPORT

All psychotherapies are partly supportive. Empirical support for this principle first appeared in one of the earliest comparative studies: Luborsky, Woody, McLellan, O'Brien, and Rosenzweig (1982). In this study, a comparison was made between three well-known but different treatments for substance abuse patients: supportive-expressive psychotherapy, cognitive-behavioral psychotherapy, and drug counseling. These three treatments were found to be virtually identical in clinician-judged degree of supportiveness. This impressively uniform finding occurs even though the SE manual is the only one of these three that accords an explicit place to the role of supportiveness. Therefore, it is noteworthy that a curative factor can exist, whether or not it is given a place in a psychotherapy treatment manual.

The sense of support may be a consequence of establishing a therapeutic relationship. After all, a patient typically initiates treatment because of problems that are disturbing her enough to wish to do something about them. It is bound to be relieving to have an ally in that quest.

EXAMPLE 1: Ms. Carrie Hopewell

A 20-year-old college student, Ms. Hopewell is in treatment for a serious eating disorder, with daily episodes of bulimia. Her history reveals a chaotic background with prominent losses—her parents divorced when she was 3, and her father died when she was 5. She is the oldest of four children.

Ms. Hopewell has difficulty making appointments and keeping a schedule. The therapist's impression is that she doesn't know how to take anything in: "She doesn't use my interpretations." One early goal of the treatment was to help her experience the therapist as on her side.

After 6 months of treatment, the patient started sobbing at the end of a session because she felt she was failing at school and would have to go home. She said she felt like a turtle in a shell, with nothing inside.

The therapist asked, "How would it be if someone were in the shell with you?" The patient nodded, indicating that she liked the idea of not being alone with her feelings. The therapist then began to talk with her about the practical problems she faced.

This example illustrates many aspects of exchanges with patients, with the main aim of establishing a supportive relationship. As forms of support, the therapist uses empathy for the patient, active efforts at enhancing the Helping Alliance, and a focus on the real elements of the patient's life.

A supportive relationship can eventually help a fragile patient feel secure enough to tolerate some degree of expressive work. While the time that it takes varies considerably, any increase opens up potential in the clinical work.

EXAMPLE 2: Ms. Carrie Hopewell

Now a junior in college, 21-year-old Carrie has made some initial, though variable, progress in treatment. She is currently back at school after a month's vacation at home. This is her first session back in therapy after the break.

P: I saw my friends. We went out. That was pretty much it. [She shrugs and looks at her nails.]

T: And being home, what was that like?

P: Not a problem, except for throwing up.

T: When did that happen?

P: Pretty much every day.

T: Seems as if it gets worse when you are at home. Have you noticed that?

P: I guess so. [She looks up at the therapist for a moment and catches her eye.]

After a year and a half of treatment, the patient is willing to hear the therapist about the links between her behavior and her life, something she could not do until she had enough experience with the therapist's support to take in her words.

PRINCIPLE 2: ESTABLISHING A "HELPING ALLIANCE" IS CRUCIAL FOR BRINGING A SENSE OF SUPPORT

The Helping Alliance is a partnership between the patient and therapist, forged around the patient's treatment needs and treatment goals. As described in chapter 7, a strong Helping Alliance is linked to positive treatment outcome (Luborsky, 1976, 2000). A Helping Alliance, type 1, in which the patient feels helped by the therapist, and a Helping Alliance, type 2, in which the sense of partnership is prominent, both bring a sense of support. Establishing a Helping Alliance can help the patient maintain hope while working through painful or difficult material.

PRINCIPLE 3: THE THERAPIST'S EMPATHIC RESPONSES CAN BE BENEFICIAL TO THE OUTCOME OF PSYCHOTHERAPY

Research indicates that the therapist's empathy is linked to a positive outcome for the treatment (Luborsky, Crits-Christoph, Mintz, & Auerbach, 1988). Empathy refers to *feeling with* the patient. It is a form of understanding that is more about the patient's affect states than about her thoughts. Translating empathy into words can deepen the alliance since it keeps the dialogue between patient and therapist quite directly at the heart of the problem.

The therapist's ability to read the patient's nonverbal cues and to notice shifts in emotional state allows the therapist to facilitate the growth of a relationship reminiscent of the early attachment between parent and child, in which the parent's ability to read and respond to an infant's cues is linked to the security of the attachment. Fonagy (2003) suggests that the links between attachment and the treatment relationship give the therapy some of its potential.

PRINCIPLE 4: THE THERAPIST SHOULD DO NOTHING TO HINDER THE DEVELOPMENT OF A POSITIVE REGARD

The therapist should not do anything that might counteract the tendency of the patient to form a positive relationship with the therapist and the treatment. Research on the Helping Alliance shows that early positive Helping Alliance signs were significant predictors of the outcome of treatment. This finding supports Freud's recommendations on the value of a positive regard: "If one exhibits a serious interest in him [the patient] . . . and avoids making certain mistakes, he will himself form such an attachment. . . . It is certainly possible to forfeit this first success if from the start one takes any standpoint other than that of sympathetic understanding" (1913a/1958, pp. 139-140). The simple stance of sympathetic understanding is of great value, especially during the first phase of psychotherapy.

PRINCIPLE 5: EVEN THOUGH THE THERAPIST'S SUPPORTIVE STATEMENTS ARE INTENDED TO BE HELPFUL, SOMETIMES THEY MAY NOT BE

In reading this section it is useful to keep this seeming paradox in mind: A therapist cannot perform these supportive techniques and assume they are received by the patient as the therapist intended. Schlesinger states this even more categorically (personal communication, 1983): "The patient has the right to define what it is that the therapist presents—it is a supportive technique if the patient experiences it as supportive."

In spite of a therapist's best efforts, misunderstandings can happen. So can negative reactions to events, words, or expressions on the part of the therapist. Negative reactions need to be noted and questioned so they do not "stay underground" and subvert the treatment. Intense and early negative reactions are more characteristic of some patients than others. They are a hallmark of patients with severe personality disorders, as Kernberg (1984) finds. But misunderstandings or unanticipated reactions can also happen in any treatment, regardless of the pathology of the patient or of the therapist.

Finding out what has gone wrong takes patience and nondefensive inquiry on the part of the therapist, but it can lead to restoration through repair of the conditions for the therapeutic alliance. It also elevates the potential for some gains from the process. In fact, the presence of cycles of "rupture and repair" is correlated with positive treatment outcome (Safran, Muran, & Walner, 1994; Safran & Muran, 1996, 2000a, 2000b; Safran, Muran, Samstag, & Stevens, 2001).

PRINCIPLE 6: THE THERAPIST MUST DECIDE WHICH PATIENTS REQUIRE ADDITIONAL STRENGTHENING OF THE SUPPORTIVE RELATIONSHIP

Patients differ considerably in the amount of support they require. For many patients in SE psychotherapy, the techniques can be mainly expressive throughout the treatment, with the supportive elements coming through the implicit support of the Helping Alliance and the structure of the treatment. But for some patients, the inherent level of supportiveness in the psychotherapy may need to be increased. Patients who do not tolerate anxiety well or patients for whom it is essential to strengthen rather than analyze defenses (Gill, 1951) are more likely to require extra support.

There are many reasons to give additional support: (1) so that the patient will feel able to manage problems that had felt overwhelming, (2) so that self-esteem is maintained, (3) so that the patient's sense of reality is backed up, (4) so that a patient's self-punishing tendencies are lessened, and (5) so that anxiety about warded-off wishes are modulated. (Examples of how and when support may be provided are offered later in the chapter.)

Often, the decision about whether and what kind of additional support is needed is clear to the therapist early in treatment and remains clear throughout. But for some patients the decision about the most appropriate treatment techniques is hard to make, as was true for Kohut's (1977) patient whom he reanalyzed more empathically.

The therapist's initial decision may be helped through evaluation of the Health-Sickness level of the patient, though questions may sometimes be answered by having the patient go through a diagnostic psychological assessment (Rapaport, Gill, & Schafer, 1968). As in medicine generally, adequate diagnosis should lead to the needed treatment and should help guide the appropriate proportion of supportive and expressive techniques (Schlesinger, 1969). Diagnostic testing can give another level of information to that process.

The therapist may use the initial treatment period to gather clinical impressions that guide those decisions. For example, the therapist may gauge the patient's responses to interventions that are just trials (Freud, 1913a/1958). Finally, the therapist's decision may come gradually, after more experience with the patient's treatment, by keeping open to the ongoing experience of the patient in treatment, as in the following examples.

EXAMPLE 1: Mr. Tom Zeman (from Kohut, 1977)

A well-known example of how hard it may be to decide how to strengthen supportive conditions is shown by Kohut's (1977) own reanalysis of his patient. In the first analysis with its poor outcome, Kohut had relied on standard expressive techniques. Dissatisfied with the results, he shifted to a more supportive approach in the second analysis by responding through empathy rather than interpretation. He used techniques such as "mirroring" to validate the patient's experience and improve his precarious self-esteem. This contrasted with the first analysis, in which many of the therapist's interpretations had been experienced by the patient as attacks on his self-worth.

EXAMPLE 2: Mr. Paul Roberts

Mr. Roberts began treatment because of anxieties at work that contributed to obsessive checking and rechecking of his office reports, as well as to working very long hours. Although he had been with his company for a only a year and a half, he had already been promoted. However, the patient believed that "if they only knew," his supervisor would discover that he (the patient) really knew nothing.

During the first several months of treatment, the therapy began to uncover this central theme: the belief that others would judge him as incompetent, leading to his need to keep proving himself. The therapist and her supervisor thought the work was going well until a day when the patient arrived unusually early for his session.

"They let the whole department go," he announced. The patient reported that his company had been bought out by a larger company, and he was abruptly out of work. He continued treatment, but the therapist began to notice that he looked disheveled and was often late for appointments. When she inquired about the lateness, he couldn't offer any explanation. Finally he admitted that now that he wasn't working, he saw no point in going to bed at night and was staying up most of the night, playing computer games. He eventually admitted that he'd let showering go, too.

In supervision, the therapist decided she needed to take a new approach. While this patient had been able to do exploratory work while he was employed, it seemed to be going nowhere now, and his life was going rapidly downhill. She decided to focus on helping him regain structure and a sense of control. First, however, she discussed the state of the treatment with the patient.

T: I was wondering whether what we are doing here is really helping you enough right now.

P: You mean now that I don't have a life?

T: Well, maybe all these grand ideas won't help as much as a job right now.

P: Well, yeah.

He began to focus more on his real-life difficulties, while the therapist shifted to supporting him in efforts to cope. This helped the patient stop his "downslide" and begin to take stock of his situation.

PRINCIPLE 7: THERAPIST FACILITATION MAY BE NEEDED TO DEVELOP THE HELPING ALLIANCE

The Helping Alliance often grows simply through the presence of the therapist and the work of the treatment. The patient will recognize that the therapist is trying to help, the patient will feel helped, and a better Helping Alliance will form. But sometimes it is not as easy as that.

Patients differ in the degree to which they can experience the presence of an alliance, due at times to the nature of their past relationships or to other factors that might lessen trust. When the development of the alliance is problematic, these 12 methods for strengthening the alliance can be useful.

Helping Alliance Method 1: Encourage the Patient's Efforts to Work toward the Goals

When the therapist offers support for the patient's efforts, through work as well as through attitude, it can strengthen the alliance. Listen to the patient and notice the ways he might be moving toward what he wants for himself, as in the following example:

EXAMPLE: Mr. Mark Anderson

T: Do you remember when you started therapy, you said that you needed to figure out why you got so anxious about even thinking of asking someone out? Well, it looks as if you've really gotten somewhere with that.

Helping Alliance Method 2: Convey Acceptance and Understanding

Acceptance can be conveyed through how the therapist listens to all the patient has to say, as well as through other nonjudgmental responses. Patients may watch the therapist's expressions. Discussion of any questions that the patient has about the therapist's attitude can further the alliance. Freud (1913a/1958) strongly recommends "sympathetic understanding" as a helpful attitude. This means that rather than preaching or saying what is right, the therapist should be listening or on the way to understanding.

Helping Alliance Method 3: Find Ways to Like the Patient

When the therapist likes the patient, it turns out to be significantly associated with the outcome of the treatment (Horvath & Symonds, 1991). It also facilitates the development of the Helping Alliance, perhaps because the patient can sense the therapist's liking. Sloane, Staples, Cristol, Yorkson, and Whipple (1975) found this correlation after 4 months of treatment. It could be that their finding shows a preference on the part of therapists for those patients who improved more. However, it seems more likely that the therapist's liking had an impact on the patient. In fact, in three out of five studies, the degree of liking was a significant predictor of outcome when the prediction was made early in treatment (Luborsky, Crits-Christoph, et al., 1988).

Helping Alliance Method 4: Support Essential Defenses and Activities

A useful form of support comes through listening for the patient's strengths. This means attending to forms of competence and effective defenses and making use of the treatment to bolster them (Gill, 1951). It also means listening for how the patient is handling the basic structures in her life, such as employment and education, and to see whether she is coping adequately. The therapist should be ready to explore whatever may get in the way of such essentials as finding a job or finishing an education. This treatment recommendation is crucial for patients who need support and encouragement to keep their lives together, especially those who are severely ill or vulnerable to regression. Some of those patients are unable to use expressive techniques, as is true for Ms. Jane Harvey.

EXAMPLE: Ms. Jane B. Harvey

Ms. Harvey has recently returned home from a brief hospitalization for an episode of severe depression. While she was sinking into the depression, she retreated from those around her. In treatment, the therapist is focusing with her on her efforts to re-engage with daily life.

P: I went to buy groceries, but when I got to the checkout, there were long lines at every counter, I mean *long*. I almost left the cart right there, but then I didn't. I waited, 'cause I thought, "I'll need this."

T: I can see that you are trying hard to do what it takes to make your life work.

Helping Alliance Method 5: Convey a Hopeful Attitude

When the therapist conveys hope, it can and usually does make a difference in the treatment. The therapist should communicate a belief in the possibility of change in general, as well as interest in achieving the patient's goals in particular. The benefits of hope have often been observed by experienced therapists (e.g., Frank, 1968; French & Wheeler, 1963; Menninger, 1942; Bergin & Lambert, 1978).

Since many patients begin treatment when their problems seem overwhelming, some degree of hopelessness is frequent. Hopelessness can make it hard for the patient to believe he will ever get better and consequently to make efforts in treatment. If the therapist conveys a sense of hopefulness, the patient will be more likely to continue to try and more likely to benefit from treatment. Research studies tend to support this thinking. Five out of seven studies found that positive expectations of the therapist are predictive of good outcomes in psychotherapy (Luborsky, McLellan, Woody, O'Brien, & Auerbach, 1985). Meta-analyses combining results of many studies support the importance of the patient's and the therapist's hopefulness about treatment outcome (Bergin & Lambert, 1978; Luborsky, Singer, & Luborsky, 1975; Smith, Glass, & Miller, 1980). These studies, along with research showing that the majority of patients do "get better," suggest that hope in psychotherapy is grounded in reason.

Helping Alliance Method 6: Acknowledge Progress in the Treatment

When the therapist acknowledges progress in the treatment, it can further the Helping Alliance. Since treatment goals are achieved through a process that often does not seem apparent to the patient, the recognition that progress is being made can be useful.

Helping patients notice the gradual steps along the way can keep them from getting needlessly discouraged. The treatment goals are achieved not in one powerful leap but, rather, by putting one foot ahead of another, with resting places along the way to get perspective on how far one has traveled. It helps in keeping up morale to point out milestones where one can look back to survey the distance one has come.

EXAMPLE 1: Ms. Sarah Satin

T: Did you notice that?

P: What?

T: You are sounding much more satisfied with your life than you seemed to be for the last 2 years.

P: [Laughs] I guess that's true.

In the SE session-limited version of psychotherapy particularly, it is useful to discuss with the patient some partial goals, since the goals may not be fully reached at the time of termination.

EXAMPLE 2: Ms. Helene Elliott

The patient selected a time-limited treatment since she was planning in a matter of months to move to Michigan for graduate school. Her goal was to be ready for a new relationship by "clearing away the cobwebs" of a painful breakup and a childhood of long periods of distance in family relationships. After two thirds of the sessions had been completed, she and the therapist agreed that she had come far on the "cobwebs" part with regard to the breakup and made a good start on the rest. When they talked over her progress, the patient was satisfied that this could be a "realistic" ending.

Helping Alliance Method 7: Make It Safe for the Patient to Express Himself

Sometimes patients are inhibited about self-expression. This may be due to an overall inhibition or to particular issues that are hard to talk about. Noting which topics seem to be linked to nonexpressiveness can help open up barriers. This could be considered as a clinical application of the Symptom-Context method, since the topic is being linked with the symptom.

Both supportive and expressive techniques come into play in helping a patient become free to express herself. The supportive principle is to set an accepting tone, to allow the patient to feel safe in the treatment. The expressive principle is to explore whatever makes the patient feel unsafe or inhibited, since that "whatever" is likely to be a key to the patient's progress in treatment. The patient's reactions to the therapist may be an aspect of the inhibition; those need to be considered as possible sources as well.

Helping Alliance Method 8: Facilitate a Partnership with the Patient

When the therapist and the patient become partners in the treatment, it can enhance the patient's efforts to solve his problems. The therapist can create a sense of partnership in the way he describes the work of the treatment as a joint effort. This is termed a Helping Alliance, type 2, in research. This form of alliance is consistent with the current *relational* thinking in psychoanalysis, which views treatment as a "two-person process" (Mitchell, 1995).

Helping Alliance Method 9: Show Respect for the Patient

When the therapist shows a genuine respect for the patient, it strengthens the Helping Alliance. This can be done through listening in ways that convey respect, as well as by the nature of the therapist's responses. The partnership is facilitated when the patient feels himself to be a valued part of it.

Helping Alliance Method 10: Welcome the Patient's Growing Competence as a Partner in the Process

As the patient develops competence in working together with the therapist, it is beneficial for the therapist to welcome her growing skills. This can further the Helping Alliance, type 2, and let the patient know she is welcome to "grow into" the same levels of understanding as the therapist—and beyond. It can also help counteract tendencies toward a hierarchical relationship, in which the patient could feel she should keep the therapist in an artificially higher position of competence than herself.

Helping Alliance Method 11: Make Reference to Shared Experiences in the Treatment

When the therapist refers to shared experiences in the treatment, he is continuing the idea that "we are in this together." Patients are sometimes surprised to be remembered; it brings with it a sense that the patient and the therapist have a history together—and that it matters.

EXAMPLE: Mr. Harry Baker

T: That reminds me of the problem you had in talking to your last boss. You and I are getting experienced in dealing with that kind of problem.

Helping Alliance Method 12: Develop an Alliance around the Search for Understanding

It may seem surprising to see the search for understanding discussed under "supportive relationships." After all, the SE manual is organized around the dichotomy between supportiveness and expressiveness, with the search for understanding being the essence of the expressive work (as discussed in the next chapter). However, when the search for understanding is a joint effort, it can enhance the sense of partnership. Becoming allies in that quest can help the patient feel both competent and supported at the same time.

SUMMARY AND DISCUSSION

In Karl Menninger's course in psychotherapy, he tried to jolt the students with a provocative educational question about SE psychotherapy: "If you had only one response to make to a patient throughout the treatment, what would it be?" The response he was looking for from his hypothetical therapist was *menschlich*, a German word that means "it's natural" or "it's human." That one-word response of *menschlich* is clearly a supportive one. It conveys a vital message of acceptance to the patient.

Being supportive tends to be beneficial to the patient: It supports the patient in making progress in psychotherapy, and it helps her feel more able to confront the past restrictions that have impeded her development. Support remains one of the important factors in predicting the outcomes of psychotherapy.

All therapies have been found to contain supportive elements, and offering support is integral to the therapist's role (as in principle 1). It is useful to evaluate the amount and forms of support the patient needs. It has been found to be of particular clinical importance with patients at the lower end of the Health-Sickness scale. Facilitating the Helping Alliance furthers the sense of support. Helping Alliance "type 1" techniques include these forms of support: by showing support for the patient and the patient's wish to reach his goals through finding ways to like the patient, by helping the patient keep up vital defenses and activities that are important for functioning, by maintaining a sense of hope that the treatment goals can be achieved, and by recognizing progress toward the goals when it occurs.

Helping Alliance "type 2" techniques include encouraging a sense of partnership, referring to experiences that the patient and therapist have been through together, and engaging in the joint search for understanding. The last is actually an expressive technique, but it has a strong supportive function as well. It conveys the message that "we are working together to overcome the problems that brought you into therapy in the first place."

Chapter Ten

Expressive Techniques: Ways of Listening and Understanding

Free expression of "what comes to mind" differentiates dynamic psychotherapy from other forms. It originates in the psychoanalytic premise that unedited material will allow both conscious and unconscious thoughts to come to light. Unlike most other forums in life, dynamic psychotherapy invites both rational and irrational thoughts. Dreams, including those from sleep and daydreams from waking life, as well as memories of the past, are all welcome material.

This open view of inner life can itself bring information. Something as simple as the confidential opportunity to speak previously unspoken thoughts can let the patient hear himself in a new way. The therapist sets the stage for expressiveness by the way she listens. When the therapist conveys interest and empathy, that facilitates the patient's ease in speaking his mind.

Clinical research supports the link of the patient's expressiveness with the outcome of treatment (Orlinsky, Grawe, & Parks, 1994). Of 51 studies examined and rated for patient expressiveness, 32 had positive significant effects on outcome, while 2 of these studies found negative significant effects, with 17 having "little effect" (nonsignificant). These combined results suggest that expressiveness has predominately positive effects on the treatment.

PROCESS IN SE PSYCHOTHERAPY

The therapist's role in the process of SE psychotherapy is composed of a repeating series of different forms of listening, understanding, and responding. While each session moves through a version of these steps, the emphasis will shift as the treatment progresses. The proportion of time and focus on each step will vary, based on the patient's current needs and the phase of the treatment.

Early treatment is typically a time for the patient to explore and express what is in her heart and on her mind. It is time for the therapist to hear the patient with an empathetic ear and with curiosity about the sources of problems and pain. Patterns in the patient's problems will begin to be visible.

Later treatment is typically the time to explore repeating problems and their sources. A deepening understanding will gradually emerge, shifting the way the patient and therapist hear the material. The patient may begin to use that understanding to make changes in his responses at any point, but the later phase gives more grounding to the changes. The basic components of expressive work, which are repeated and expanded throughout the treatment, are summarized in figure 10.1.

Listening is the therapist's first essential task in every session. "Being heard" is achieved when the therapist has an "open ear" and the patient has moved through any obstacles in the way of believing that he can be heard.

Understanding is a gradual and continual process achieved through hearing the patterns of problems the patient presents—along with their contexts—both past and present. The CCRT and the Symptom-Context method both give frameworks that can clarify the emerging patterns.

Responding occurs when the therapist shares a gist of his understanding of the patient, timed to fit with the patient's own emerging understanding. In that way, early responses may be more likely to be about the immediate problems and the affect around them, while later responses will be more likely to include an understanding of a pattern.

Listening again follows the therapist's response. After the therapist speaks, the space and time belong to the patient. The therapist's responses should not dominate the session. The therapist attends to how the patient uses what she has offered, as well as what fresh material the patient may bring.

Figure 10.1. The basic components of expressive work.

The process of the expressive work is one of exploring patterns, meanings, and their previously hidden sources. This chapter focuses on the early phase of the process of listening and understanding. One goal of the early phase of expressive work is for the patient to develop an interest in the search. The therapist can facilitate that engagement by noticing and appreciating the patient's efforts at understanding.

EXAMPLE: Ms. Mary Cunningham

When Ms. Cunningham began treatment, she spoke in a monotone. Nothing had any more importance than anything else. But after 3 months in treatment, she is beginning to become more curious about her feelings and their sources.

P: I was taking a shower, and I started thinking about back then. You know, it's like everything goes dark.

T: Really wanting to know what was happening back then.

P: Yeah. I know it wasn't good. . . .

When the patient and therapist share in the search, it strengthens the Helping Alliance and facilitates the patient's engagement in the process of the treatment.

WAYS OF LISTENING

1. Open Listening

Open listening means listening fresh, with an open mind and attuned senses, to what the patient brings. Rather than listening for a specific problem or symptom, this form of listening corresponds to what Freud (1912b/1958) referred to as "evenly suspended" attention. He makes this recommendation for the therapist: "He should simply listen and not bother about whether he is keeping anything in mind" (Freud, 1912b/1958, p. 112). Open listening is of particular importance at the beginning of sessions, when the therapist should set aside any earlier formulation about the patient and listen anew.

The fact that SE psychotherapy is a form of *dynamic* treatment does not mean the therapist should try to fit what the patient says into any particular kind of dynamics. That would risk making the patient fit into a theory rather than keeping open to what she has to say. It is after the therapist has heard the patient that he can consider how to understand the meaning, including how it may correspond to a particular theory. In that way, listening to the patient comes before any concept.

2. Listening for the Affect

Patients come to treatment because something is bothering them, very often causing considerable distress. The therapist will want to listen to the affect itself, in order to "read" the patient's level of pain. Listening for the emotional story involves attuning to *the feel of* a patient's communication. The therapist may gain a viseral sense of the patient's emotional states through this form of listening. When the affect and the content do not match, that discordance will be another source of information.

The therapist will also need to listen for which themes or situations are linked to the most affect. Both the nature of the feeling state and the possible triggers for those feelings matter in gaining a sense of the patient's emotional life.

3. Listening for Patterns and Their Sources

As the therapist listens, he may begin to notice patterns in the patient's symptoms and the stories in which they are embedded. As the treatment unfolds, repeating patterns will stand out more clearly, especially as the therapist tunes his ear to listen for the CCRT components in relationship episodes.

As described in the chapter on the CCRT (chapter 4), the therapist will listen to the patient's stories about himself in relation to others to determine his CCRT components. What responses does the patient tend to expect from other people? Are there certain kinds of negative experiences that recur? Are there self-defeating responses that may be part of a pattern? What did he really wish for, underneath the pain and the problems?

Sometimes one or more of the elements are implied, not stated. As a clincial method, the CCRT is tailor-made for each patient. It is not a set pattern that the therapist knows and applies to the patient. It emerges from listening to the patient's own story.

Events from childhood can be especially helpful in grounding the treatment because they yield clues to some early relationship experiences that may have been formative. Listen for themes of attachment, for repeated or prolonged separations, and for experiences of loss (Bowlby, 1988). Abuse, trauma, or high-conflict relationships are also important to uncover. Each of these forms of experience may make its way into current symptoms or relationship problems.

4. Listening for the Triggers and Context of Symptoms

Along with listening for the elements of the CCRT pattern, the therapist will be listening for the triggers and context of symptoms. Clues to the function and meaning of a symptom can be gleaned from the surrounding events and the feelings associated with them. As described in the chapter on the Symptom-Context method (chapter 5), that form of listening can yield a joint quest for understanding of symptoms as they emerge.

Listening for events or reactions that appear to set off a symptom allows the patient and therapist to notice its possible meanings. Traumatic events that have been remembered in only a fragmentary form can gain more coherence through this form of listening, as in this example:

EXAMPLE: Ms. Patricia Cutter Halifax

P: Woke up with a migraine this morning. Seems like it's worse on Tuesday [the day of her session].

T: What do you think that's about?

P: Could be because of talking about *him*.

This patient has been coming to terms with early sexual abuse for several years. At this point she is linking the symptoms with their discovered context herself.

5. Listening to Check on the Accuracy of the Therapist's Understanding

A different type of listening is needed when the therapist wants to see whether a hypothesis is accurate. At these times, the therapist listens again to hear how the patient's statements correspond to the therapist's *working understanding* of the patient. For example, the therapist may be formulating the CCRT pattern but also listening to hear whether the formulation is adequate. Such relistening can confirm or amend the therapist's hypotheses, helping the therapist guard against being too quick to arrive at a formulation about the patient.

In session-limited psychotherapy, the therapist will need to go ahead with her formulation after several sessions, due to time constraints. However, in open-ended therapies, the therapist should continue to relisten so as to keep her understanding of the patient linked as accurately as possible with the patient's material. Even where relistening confirms the essential pattern, the therapist's understanding of the patient will be enriched by hearing more of the obstacles and ordeals that the patient has faced.

In essence, listening, in all of these forms, is vital to the first phase of SE psychotherapy. It yields the material that forms the crux of the meanings to be discovered.

WAYS OF UNDERSTANDING

Gaining understanding is a gradual process, one that requires patience on the part of both patients and therapists. The evolution of understanding takes place throughout the treatment. The therapist will listen to accounts of the patient's symptoms, conflicts, and emotional states, with an ear toward themes they may have in common.

EXAMPLE: Ms. Johanna M. Forbes

P: I was always on the outskirts, watching everybody else get picked. You know those times in grade school where you are the worst one and no one wants you on their team.

T: [Nods and listens. The therapist is wondering whether this is part of a relevant pattern. Since it is early in the treatment and she is not sure, she does not remark on that. Later in the session the patient starts talking about work. This time the therapist does speak, encouraging the patient to take the topic further.]

P: So I didn't say anything. Didn't want to stick my neck out.

T: Didn't want to stand out. Wonder what felt dangerous about that?

P: Oh, rejection, of course. Didn't want them to be thinking, "Who do you think you are?"

Now the patient has arrived at a prime theme herself, one that may begin the process of understanding her CCRT pattern.

In the beginning phase, the therapist develops hunches about the meanings of the material, as with Ms. Johanna Forbes. The different forms of listening that were described in the previous section are essential preliminaries for attaining greater understanding.

PRINCIPLES GUIDING UNDERSTANDING

Principle 1: Attend to Each Sphere of the "Relationship Triad"

Noticing the different spheres of the patient's relationship theme gives a multidimensional view of its pattern. Following are the three spheres of the *relationship triad*:

1. The important relationships in the patient's life, including those with family, friends, and colleagues
2. The past relationships with parents and other family or family-like members
3. The relationship between the patient and therapist

The therapist shifts attention between the three spheres as the material emerges (Menninger & Holzman, 1973). Recognizing the relationship pattern in different spheres helps the patient come to terms with its pervasiveness, as in the example that follows.

EXAMPLE: Mr. Michael Lantana

The patient, a graduate student in his late 20s, began treatment due to obsessional symptoms and difficulties in forming lasting relationships. The eldest child of a large family fraught with conflict, he has moved across the country and kept little contact with them.

In the current session, the patient had to walk up seven flights of stairs to the therapist's office because the elevator was out of service. The therapist noted that he was out of breath when he came in the door.

T: What was that like, having to walk up all those stairs?

P: Why are you asking such a mundane question? That is not why I come here.

T: Sounds like it is unwelcome for me to express concern.

P: It is infantilizing. As if I don't know how to climb up stairs, or something. . . . OK, it reminds me of something that happened when I was still living back home. My youngest brother fell off of his bike, he must have been 6 years old already, and he ran in to tell my mother. Ridiculous! He was too old for that.

T: It stayed with you, that he wanted help from your mother when you thought he was already too old to get help.

P: [Raises his eyebrows]

T: And I guess that seemed as ridiculous as my asking about climbing up all those stairs.

The therapist has linked the patient's defense against receiving help, in both the sphere of the therapy and that of a past experience. The childhood example doubtless has more behind it, as does his intense aversion to being seen as "infantile." But the therapist is staying with the material that the patient brings.

As in this example, it is not necessary to attend to all three spheres in the same session, although it can be useful from time to time. What is important is to notice elements of the CCRT in each relationship as they emerge. In the early phases of understanding, each element is its own discovery. Over time, the convergence of the pattern will itself be news. The overlap among the three spheres is called the "redundancy of the theme," and the content of the overlap helps in discerning what is central to the CCRT. (See figure 10.2.)

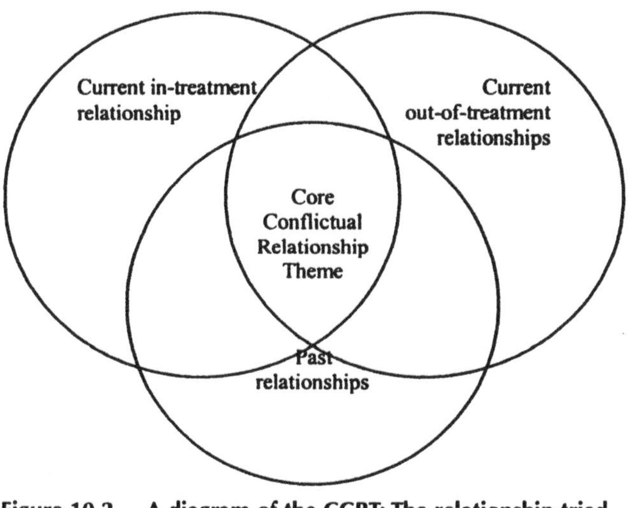

Figure 10.2. A diagram of the CCRT: The relationship triad.

Principle 2: Understand Each Relationship Sphere

Of the three spheres, the relationship between the patient and therapist may have the most therapeutic impact because it takes place in the "here and now" (Gill, 1979). Since the treatment relationship tends to activate central relational issues, the ups and downs experienced with the therapist offer the patient a good arena for the resolution of his relationship problems. In fact, if the patient seems unusually upset, and if the distress appears to have started in one of the sessions, its cause might be found in some aspect of the therapeutic relationship. Exploring such reactions can offer an *in vivo* understanding of aspects of the patient's CCRT.

Problems in current relationships are often an accessible avenue toward understanding the CCRT. Patients typically feel distress about difficulties in that sphere, making it an arena that patients are motivated to solve. Relationships with significant others are frequently sources of intense yearnings (W), as well as expectations from the other person (RO) and intense personal reactions (RS). Having the CCRT in mind can facilitate the therapist's search for the sources of relationship conflict or disappointment.

Patients vary in how much they remember from childhood, but finding out about the patient's past provides important background to current problems, especially when it involves early attachments. While there is rarely a one-to-one correspondence between past and present, the patient and therapist can examine the ways the current CCRT is linked to the past, thereby gaining greater understanding and mastery.

When the commonality between each of these three spheres—the current relationship with the therapist, the current relationships outside of treatment, and the related early relationships—is uncovered, the patient and therapist will have come a long way in understanding the transference pattern.

Principle 3: Consider the Real Aspects of the Patient's Reactions to the Therapist

The patient's responses to the therapist are rarely based on entirely false perceptions, despite the restriction of seeing the therapist through the lens of her CCRT. The therapist's characteristics and behavior may often be seen accurately, even though the patient might interpret them in ways that are consistent with her CCRT pattern. The relative contribution of the patient and of the therapist to the patient's perception varies from occasion to occasion, as well as from patient to patient. The "stimulus value" of the therapist's behavior can prove to be a valuable lead, as in this example.

EXAMPLE: Ms. Paula Longstrech

The patient is late for the session.

P: Sorry I'm late. No reason. I just lost track of time.

[The therapist is wondering, however, if the patient might not have been reacting to the therapist's own lateness the week before. She decides to share this with the patient.]

T: Do you remember last week I was running late, and we started the session about 10 minutes late?

P: Whatever. I don't care about those things.

T: OK, but I just wonder if it had some meaning to you after all, since this week it was harder to get here on time.

P: You mean like it didn't matter to you whether I was waiting?

By acknowledging her own lateness, the therapist was able to open up an area that the patient had kept out of full awareness.

Principle 4: Recognize That the Symptoms of Each Patient Become More Understandable through Their Contexts

A symptom is defined here, as in Freud (1926/1959), as a dysfunction of a usually intact function. For example, momentary forgetting is a dysfunction of memory in the sense that we usually have little problem remembering what we intend to say—normally, our memory works correctly. Episodes of momentary forgetting are fairly common during psychotherapy sessions, as are the emergence of feelings of anxiety and shifts toward increased depression. Clinical-quantitative research with the Symptom-Context method (Luborsky, 1996) supports our recommendation to pay attention to the context of the symptoms, and to their related affects, as clues to expanded understanding.

Symptoms can encode meaning in a highly condensed way. Using the context to notice what set off a symptom gives valuable information about the symptom's meaning. The obvious basis for this focus is that the patient wants help with symptoms that cause pain and suffering. The gradual understanding of a symptom will optimally allow it to take the form of words and feelings, rather than remain in its previous form.

When a symptom appears in a session, the patient and therapist will want to give special attention to the material preceding the symptom. That includes not only the spoken material but also the patient's reactions or unspoken thoughts. After the therapist and patient focus their attention on the context, they will again note the symptom and try to understand how the context and symptom may be connected.

EXAMPLE: Mr. Warren List

In this example, the therapist and patient use the Symptom-Context method to decode an episode of momentary forgetting that occurred within the session.

P: I just forgot what I was about to say. I hate it when that happens!

T: [Waits]

P: What did I just say?

T: What is the last thing you remember?

P: I was talking about work . . . the staff meeting . . . oh, I know what it was. Now that I think of it, it is rather insignificant. But at the meeting I *had* intended to bring up an idea I had for the department, only Mike kept moving the agenda along, and there was no time for me to say something.

T: Insignificant . . . I wonder if you were concerned that I would think that was insignificant?

P: Sure. But I think so too.

T: Well, if we were both going to think it was insignificant, I guess your brain edited it out before we got to it.

P: [Chuckles]

T: But I imagine it was disappointing to lose your opportunity to speak your mind at the meeting.

P: [Nods] I did have an idea for the department, if they would ever listen to me.

This Symptom-Context exchange illustrates the link between the symptom and the patient's CCRT. Feeling unheard and unimportant in the meeting was linked to avoiding such reactions from the therapist. This led to silencing himself, which was probably an element in his moderately depressed mood. The small episode of momentary forgetting offered large potential for understanding the inner workings of the patient's symptom and CCRT.

Principle 5: Understand the Languages of Behavior, Fantasy, and Dreams

Understanding of the patient's core conflicts will emerge not only through what he says about his problems but also through the nature of his behavior, fantasies, and dreams. Each of these sources can be "read" for clues to the patient's inner feelings and conflicts.

Behavior speaks by showing something about the patient and her problems. For example, the patient may be frequently late for sessions. Instead of assuming the meaning of that particular behavior, the therapist will wait to understand. Are there "real" reasons? (Such as highway construction?) Reasons that have to do with the fabric of the patient's life? (Trying to fit a session time into an overcrowded schedule?) Or do the reasons say something about how the patient feels about the therapy, perhaps as a symbol of obligations to others? Allowing the meanings to emerge requires keeping an open eye as well as an open ear. The topic becomes a fruitful one when the therapist neither prejudges nor closes it off as a possible source of meaning.

Daydreams, or fantasies, add another language to the treatment. Being able to imagine gives visuals to the patient's inner world. Daydreams often contain a wish that is too buried to see in daily life—the wish for love or for appreciation, perhaps. Fantasy gives a fanciful form to the wish. Some patients are not able to imagine, either because they are tied to the mundane or because of traumatic residue. Asking about any images that come to mind can help open up that form of processing.

Dreams offer a route to less conscious aspects of the self. Freud's "royal road to the unconscious" is still open. Dreams can offer an understanding of hopes and fears in the patient's inner life, in the language of an inner movie. Freud's description of the mechanisms of the dream, in chapter 6 of *The Interpretation of Dreams* (Freud, 1900/1953) describes his understanding of the nonlogical structures that may be present in dreams.

By coming up with associations to elements of the dream, patients can use the dream as a source of further understanding. Many patients may need a prompt to learn to associate to dreams. A simple statement such as "What comes to mind about that?" or "Does that remind you of anything?" can help a patient begin. The dream elements and dream as a whole may be used for the images and associations that help the patient and therapist with their understanding.

EXAMPLE: Mr. Brad Zimmerman

P: I had this dream last night. Really random stuff.

T: What kind of random stuff?

P: Like these people bungee jumping off a tall building. I mean insanely tall. [Laughs]

T: Well, let's see what comes to mind about "insanely tall."

After associating to the two remembered elements in the dream (the building and bungee jumping), the patient realized that the building reminded him of his office building, which was tall in size and "insanely tall" in expectations.

P: I guess I'm looking for some more freedom.

The young man in this example was in his first job out of college, where he had been experiencing anxiety episodes that interfered with his work. He was able to use the dream to explore feelings about his job, revisit his CCRT theme of feeling trapped by the expectations of others, and become clearer about his wish for more freedom.

Dreams also offer an approach to problems that a patient may be reluctant to bring up. Sexuality and aggression may appear in dream themes, opening up warded-off topics for some patients.

Dreams can be reliably judged by using the CCRT as a research method (Luborsky & Crits-Christoph, 1998). Dream-based and narrative-based CCRT's show agreement, lending support to the use of dreams as a clinical method of understanding.

Principle 6: Use Shifts and Redundancy of Themes as Clues to Understanding

When the patient abruptly shifts from one affect state to another, that may offer a clue to a triggering thought or reaction to explore. The therapist may be able to infer a possible disruption in the patient's emotional world through such a shift, which gives the patient and therapist an *in vivo* opportunity to understand the patient's core conflicts. Shifts in topic can also provide clues to underlying emotional meaning. Listening for the emotional links in the sequence of the topics may further the therapist's understanding of the patient's CCRT.

The following three telling examples of relationship patterns and their sources (Luborsky, 1984) illustrate the way shifts in emotional state help bring out the CCRT themes. They also show how the "redundancy of the theme" helps in discerning what is central to the CCRT. As described in the first principle guiding understanding, the overlap among the three spheres—that of family, current relationships, and the therapeutic relationship—creates the central sphere of overlap.

EXAMPLE 1: Mr. Peter Quinn

Three brief consecutive examples are given here for Mr. Peter Quinn, a 23-year-old veterinary student whose main symptom is recurrent depression. The beauty of having a sequence of examples from a single patient, each centered around an easily recognized nodal point (depressive mood shifts), is the heightened clarity with which the relationship theme emerges when the clinician notes its redundancy, as in Luborsky (1996). After the examples, some inferences will be drawn about the relationship theme in depressive episodes.

The first two examples follow, with identification of the shift in mood. Note the patient's words in the segments before and after a shift.

P: But she . . . she . . . so I mean . . . but I dreamt about her. You know it wasn't . . . it wasn't any special kind of dream, I mean, it was just, uh, you know, I mean it was . . . I don't remember what it was, but it wasn't anything remarkable and there was no sex in it and there was no . . . I don't know, we were just talking or something or something like that. **SHIFT POINT** *So that . . . that just made me a little tight. I don't know why.* [Voice drops] **END SHIFT POINT**

T: What made you tight? Just now?

P: Talking about her. Yeah.

T: Can you catch what was starting to make you tight?

P: No, I don't remember.

T: Was it what you said or what you thought?

P: Just the thought of her I guess. Oh, I know what it was, you know, I've got it.

T: Uhhuh.

P: It was that I said, well, a guy like me could be with her but, you know, a million times stronger. Eh, you know, as if it's me, then I'm not strong enough. That's what bothered me.

T: Yes.

P: You know. Sort of I . . . I mean, so I mean, I know you know that that's what she is and that's it, you know, unless some unfor—uh, tragedy happens to her th—you know for some reason she weakens then, but that's why I feel bad 'cause it means I—she's stronger than me, or brighter than me.

EXAMPLE 2: Mr. Peter Quinn

P: This girl that works in the library, the divorcée. I mean, we're just going to lunch. And, uh, you know, that . . . that's bad 'cause, I mean, you know, she's a sexually experienced woman and, uh, you know, I imagine she enjoys it, you know, and what am I gonna do, you know, what . . . what if she loves me. I mean, cause I think she does. I mean, you know, she thinks . . . she thinks I'm nice, you know. So I don't know [pause] sort of a problem [yawn]. But [exhale] [pause]. **SMALL SHIFT POINT** *Now what, huh? I don't know what to do or . . .* [Voice fades] **END SHIFT POINT**

T: At that moment it feels as if there's not gonna be anything else that'll come through your mind that, that you—

P: Well, it sort of—

T: —were gonna say—

P: —makes me feel bad.

T: What does?

P: When I don't have anything to say, nothing now. I don't know why. You know this guy Bullitt [voice brightens]—on depression? . . . [Long pause] [Low voice] So now what? I don't . . . I don't have anything to say. [Clears throat] [Pause]

In this example, the patient stops near a small shift in affect and says, "I don't know what to do," and begins to get depressed. The therapist inquires and finds that the patient is blaming himself because he (the patient) has nothing to say. The patient is angry at himself for not talking and then gets depressed because it means to him that he is not performing, which makes him feel inadequate. He feels unable to deal with "the divorcée." The patient is close to the idea also of talking about a similar problem in the relationship with the therapist. The patient tries to bridge the distance with the therapist by asking whether the therapist knows a man he knows, "this guy Bullitt." The problem is that the patient feels, despite what he talks about, that he will not get any recognition from the therapist.

EXAMPLE 3: Mr. Peter Quinn

This final example shows the same sequence of the therapist's listening, followed by understanding the context of the shift in the symptom of depression. The therapist's responses again point to a similar version of the CCRT:

P: Well, I don't know. I probably just felt bad about it. I didn't want to fight with him [the patient's father].

T: That's exactly what you did. You felt that you had to feel bad every time you thought of sticking him on his ass.

P: Yeah, but I never did.

T: You never did but you often wanted to.

P: Hey, no, I don't think I ever did wa—think of . . . y'know, I don't, I mean, there was never anything to fight about. Well there was . . . reasons to fight . . . okay, I guess I am s—. I hate 'im now sometimes but [sigh], I mean, he never did a damn thing. He was useless. He made money. I mean, all right, I will consider him within the . . . his historical milieu and, and, blah-blah-blah and [economic] depressions and not having anything to eat and all that shit. . . . But I . . . I . . . I don't know. **SHIFT POINT** *This . . . this just confuses me. This isn't doing me too much good.* **END SHIFT POINT**

T: Why not?

P: I don't know, 'cause I don't feel good now again.

T: Well what was—what did you say that made you not feel good right then?

P: 'Cause I just got all black and depressed again when I wasn't, I was out 10 percent then.

T: That's right, you were. Then catch what made you feel all depressed again.

P: Something about my father, I guess.

T: Yes?

P: I don't know. I was fighting him or something.

T: Yes.

P: That I hated him.

T: Yes. Yes.

P: Why I had to feel guilty about—

T: Yes.

P: —hating him?

T: Yes.

P: Well, I guess you do. You have to love your father, and all that shit.

T: Right. Yeah. And so if you hate him and you feel like fighting him and setting him on his ass, then you have to feel depressed about the whole damn thing.

P: And it's—therefore I feel that way with all males.

T: Including this male talking with you.

P: Yes.

In summary, this patient was depressed but had gradually begun to come out of it until the point in the third example marked *shift point* when the patient got depressed again. The therapist noted the shift and then tried to understand the context for this shift. What was revealed was that before the shift the patient was angry at his father because he felt that his father was less than he should be and could not be admired. Just before the shift, the patient seemed to begin to feel guilty about his anger at his father.

This relationship theme became clearer after more examples were examined. The three examples typically involve comparing himself with another person. Then he often felt inadequate and decided that the other person was inadequate. In the first example, the shift in depressive mood came after the thought "I'm not strong enough" to compete with the guy for the girl. In the second example, the shift came when he compared himself with a more sexually experienced person than he was.

The essence of the main relationship theme can now be stated as it is in the CCRT formulation. In all three of these examples for Mr. Quinn, and in other examples from the same patient, the most frequent relationship themes as expressed in the first person follow:

WISH (W): "I want to feel I am adequate in comparison with another person, usually a man."
RESPONSE FROM OTHERS (RO): "You are inadequate."
RESPONSE OF SELF (RS): "I feel painfully convinced of being inadequate. Sometimes I put down someone else, like my father, and then I become depressed."

In essence, this formulation connects the content of the main symptom with its main context.

SUMMARY AND DISCUSSION

Expressive techniques are multifaceted. They allow patients an opportunity to be heard while gaining increasing awareness of their experiences. Expressive techniques are the prime source of material to guide the search for understanding. The process of reaching an understanding is helped by searching for redundancy in the three central spheres of treatment: the therapeutic relationship, current relationships outside the treatment, and early-in-life central relationships.

The CCRT is a convenient and reliable tool for understanding the themes in a patient's relationships. It can be applied during a session, as explained here and in greater detail in chapter 4. A wealth of findings have shown the CCRT to bring validity to the understanding of a patient's inner life.

Understanding symptoms in their context is another part of expressive work. Symptoms that occur during therapy, such as momentary forgetting of a particular thought, provide opportunities to understand the patient's core conflicts and their consequences. Chapter 5 describes the research behind this method, along with its clinical applications.

The listening and understanding of the first phase of treatment carries the patient and therapist into shared understandings of patterns and problems in the patient's life. The next chapter deals with how the therapist may make use of that understanding in responding to the patient.

Chapter Eleven

Expressive Techniques: Ways of Responding

In SE psychotherapy, the therapist's response is not in itself considered the cure for the patient's problems. Instead, it is one of the steps in the series of different forms of listening, understanding, responding, and listening anew. This makes the response part of a shared discovery process, where the patient and the therapist collaborate in finding out the core conflicts that underlie the patient's problems.

The therapist shifts from listening to responding in order to share with the patient *some* of what he has understood so far. How much of the understanding is conveyed is less important than saying it in a way that is likely to reach the patient. Sometimes the response will be the therapist's reflections on what the patient has been saying, and at other times the response will be a question, to clarify or deepen the material. In either case, it grows out of what the patient brings to the session on that day. "Less is more" makes a useful principle for the length of the therapist's response. In the later phase of treatment, the patient and therapist have already gained an initial view of the CCRT and its workings. Here they will review the elements in different contexts so that the patient gains a sharper awareness of their presence in his life. After the patient has gained sufficient familiarity with the ways his CCRT pattern operates and how it stops him from reaching his goals, he can begin to think about and experiment with shifting the negative aspects of that pattern. A process of change takes place as the patient finds new ways to respond to the same kinds of difficulties, ones that do not thwart his wishes or cause as many untoward consequences.

In general, the therapist's response has several different functions. One is to further the Helping Alliance by conveying empathy, as described in the chapter on the supportive relationship (chapter 9). Another is to further the expressive work by clarifying the patient's CCRT, along with its role in the patient's symptoms. The accuracy of the therapist's responses in relation to the patient's core themes does matter, as supported by research on facets of interpretation in dynamic treatment (Piper, Joyce, McCallum, & Azim, 1993). This appears to be unrelated to the effects of the Helping Alliance (Luborsky & Crits-Christoph, 1998), suggesting that they affect the treatment in different ways.

In order to respond with accuracy, the therapist needs to become adept both at listening and at pattern recognition. Responding during the expressive work is facilitated by the SE principles that follow. Of these principles of responding, numbers 1, 2, and 3 are the most fundamental of the set.

PRINCIPLES OF RESPONDING: FUNDAMENTAL PRINCIPLES

Principle 1: Point Out the Workings of the CCRT

1. *The pivotal responses in each session point to the workings of the patient's CCRT, often one strand at a time.* While the patient tells stories of the problems in her life, the CCRT is embedded in those stories (or relationship episodes). As described in chapter 4 on the CCRT method, the therapist engages in a process that is like tracking a red thread across a field. The red thread is the patient's CCRT, which is composed of three strands: the wish, the expected or experienced responses from others, and the responses of the self. The therapist's responses should highlight each strand as it emerges, so that the patient begins to gain familiarity with the pivotal workings of the strands. The red thread is often invisible, but when it comes into view the therapist may welcome it as a rediscovery that can further the process of understanding.
2. *Each of the therapist's responses should follow from material the patient brings so that the responses are in tune with the patient's current concerns.* The responses should also be observations that are close enough to his awareness to make sense to him. In other words, it should be an observation that the patient is ready to hear, not something that is too heavily defended against at this time in the treatment (Bibring, 1954; Glover, 1955).

Principle 2: Link the Symptoms with Their Contexts

When a symptom appears in the session, the therapist should pay particular attention to that event and draw it to the patient's attention in an empathic manner. The therapist will want to inquire about its context by asking about thoughts or feelings that might have preceded the symptom, unless the patient brings up this material herself. The patient and therapist can then engage in a discovery process of the meanings of the symptom.

The "symptom" refers not only to major symptoms but also to components of those symptoms, as well as to related dysfunctions. For example, a patient who has come to treatment due to a depressed mood may show a drop in mood during the session that is not a relapse into the full state of depression. The therapist should note the change in mood so that the patient and therapist can work on the kinds of triggers that set off his problems.

This takes place in the treatment of Mr. Peter Quinn, whose sessions were detailed in full in the previous chapter. That treatment illustrates both principle 1, of clarifying the CCRT themes, and principle 2, of noting the symptom in its context. The three samples from Mr. Quinn's psychotherapy are discussed here in order to illustrate how to use these pivotal principles together in treatment.

EXAMPLE: Mr. Peter Quinn

Mood shifts: The therapist points attention to the patient's shift in mood when it occurs. That helps the patient discover the thoughts that were connected to the downward shift. In the first sample, the patient links the shift to feeling inadequate, as he compares his ability to get a positive response from a woman with that of another man. This forms a part of the patient's CCRT, of which he now has some awareness.

The CCRT: In the second sample, the therapist responds again by noting the patient's shift in mood. At this point the patient begins to realize the "self" component of his CCRT is "I have nothing to say, and therefore I'm bad." The therapist responds by inquiring about the link between having nothing to say and the self-blame evident in his comment "I'm bad."

The symptom and the CCRT: In the third sample, the therapist draws attention to the patient's shift in mood. When the therapist asks about the basis for the linkage, the patient realizes he is angry at his father because of his father's being inadequate, yet he then feels bad about being angry at his father. That set of thoughts leads to the return of his symptom of depression.

This series of three episodes illustrates that after the therapist responded by noting the shift in the patient's depression, related CCRT themes began to emerge. This is also illustrated in the shift during the second example, where he attributes his sense of inadequacy to his not speaking. This idea is even more clearly spelled out in the third example, where the other person, his father, is seen as inadequate: The patient's inadequacy is attributed both to his father's and to the therapist's inadequacy. These people, he thinks, deprive him of being able to feel more adequate. The different spheres of his CCRT pattern have now emerged.

The example of Mr. Peter Quinn illustrates how the therapist responds to a patient whose symptoms appear within the sessions. Patients often need help with symptoms that do not appear within the treatment setting as well. The therapist can work with those symptoms, and their contexts, as the patient reports them. The symptoms may also be understood in relation to the patient's history, through stories of early relationship problems.

Principle 3: "Work Through" the Meaning of the CCRT

After the therapist has pointed out the components of the CCRT, and the ways it may emerge through symptoms, the therapeutic work is still not complete. In order for change to take place, the patient needs to come to terms with the ways this core theme intrudes on his life and on what he wishes for himself. This is part of the concept of "working through" that was brought out first in Freud's paper "Remembering, Repeating and Working Through" (Freud, 1914/1958). What the patient learns in psychotherapy comes out of the process of working through the CCRT themes.

A crucial gain takes place through this process. The same theme that has previously been expressed in symptoms and behavior is now able to be understood and expressed in words. This is the foundation of the transformation process that takes place in a successful treatment.

Here is a summary of essential gains through the CCRT process:

1. After experience in treatment, the patient learns to recognize cues to the CCRT pattern that help him decode its presence.
2. The patient becomes more aware of the effect of the CCRT on his relationships and symptoms.
3. The patient comes to terms with the origins of the problem.
4. The patient develops new ways of coping with previously conflictual relationship issues. After working through the CCRT pattern, the patient is able to alter his expected responses from others and his own previously maladaptive responses. This gives him new skill in coping, as well as mastery over his CCRT pattern.

PRINCIPLES OF RESPONDING: THE THERAPEUTIC RELATIONSHIP

Principle 4: Remember That Patients Often Find It Difficult to Express Thoughts about Their Therapists

In spite of the recommendation made here and elsewhere to attend to problems in the patient-therapist relationship, this is often the hardest part of the CCRT to deal with for both the patient and therapist, resulting in a tendency to avoid the topic. Freud (1912a/1958) considers the patient's role in the partial avoidance of this issue: "For it is evident that it becomes particularly hard to admit to any proscribed wishful impulse that has to be revealed in front of the very person to whom the impulse relates" (p. 104).

In spite of such obstacles, efforts to understand problems within the patient-therapist relationship can bring considerable potential for growth. Reactions to the therapist that are consistent with his core problems outside of the treatment are sometimes thought of as "transference tests," since the patient is facing what has been a habitual and formidable obstacle. When the patient succeeds in feeling understood, he gains through having "confronted the lion." When both patient and therapist are both participants and witnesses in the process of untangling the problem, it has a powerful effect.

When the therapist presents a case in supervision, or reflects on the process, any blocks to dealing with the treatment relationship become rather quickly apparent. This is not necessarily due to greater knowledge on the part of the supervisor but to the relative ease in seeing patterns when standing back from the situation. Whether the patient is "testing" the therapist, or any other form of intense interpersonal engagement, it can become more difficult for the therapist to maintain both the engagement and the objectivity to understand the process. For that reason, some form of supervision or personal review can be helpful at those times.

EXAMPLE: Mr. Henry Thorne

The patient spoke about his "bête noire," that every woman he gets involved with needs so much of his time that he cannot get done what he needs to do for himself.

P: I was trying to leave, but she kept on pleading with me to stay. She gets this pout on, saying she really needs me there, and I'm stuck.

T: Sounds as if you really feel caught by her needs.

P: [Nods] Even though she knows I have so much work to catch up on, she pleads for me to stay. It reminds me of Juliana, you know, I ended up living with her because she hated being alone. . . . She was a beautiful woman, but I just never got a minute to myself.

T: With both of these women, you ended up feeling trapped by *their* needs.

The therapist heard the patient expressing his core theme: feeling that he had to take care of the needs of others while feeling frustrated that they did not respect his own needs. Her responses to the patient remained with that theme.

As soon as she presented the material in supervision, she heard a thought that she hadn't considered before: that the patient might experience the relationship with her in the treatment in a similar way. She made a mental note to listen for its appearance in the subsequent sessions. After all, coming to treatment is a commitment of time, and the patient could at any point begin to feel that it was for the therapist's needs, rather than for his own.

Research supports the clinical impression that it is indeed more difficult for the therapist to respond to issues in the therapeutic relationship when the issues are described more abstractly. This is shown by the "match of messages" test (described later in this chapter) and by the rating scales for the therapist's responses. Ratings on these scales indicate this tendency in such items as "the degree to which the therapist's response passes the patient's test" or "the degree to which the therapist's response is directed to the most emotion-laden part of the patient's transference pattern in the session." A means of estimating the quality of the therapist's response to the patient's experience of the relationship comes through the research of Gill and Hoffman (1982), while research that focuses on the degree to which the therapist passes the patient's tests comes through the work of Weiss and Sampson (1986).

Avoiding the topic of the relationship with the therapist can come either from not having been aware of the problem or from concerns about possible negative fallout should the problem be raised. For the first problem, if the therapist spends time gaining fluency in using the CCRT, it will sharpen his awareness of the central theme being expressed in relation to him. That sharpened awareness is also helped by seeing the treatment relationship as a sphere, where the CCRT pattern is likely to emerge no matter where one starts.

For the second type of problem, it is useful for the therapist to think out or talk out the dilemma. Concerns about how to phrase the issue may be due to a sense that the theme is a "touchy topic" for the patient—or for the therapist. In other words, the therapist needs to consider both the transference and countertransference reactions to find likely sources of the problem.

Sometimes the therapist will come to the conclusion that her reluctance to bring up the problem was justified, since some patients seem more able to tolerate such discussion than others. With some patients, the likelihood that this would be experienced as a slight or criticism is so high that the therapist may continue to listen, respond, and wait until the topic seems more "talkable." Sometimes the patient does seem not to be ready for the topic because it is not close to his awareness.

Principle 5: Respond Carefully to "Tests" of the Therapeutic Relationship

Some patients need to find out how similar the therapist is to other disappointing or traumatizing figures from his past. Since treatment activates such relational patterns, that revival can bring with it the need to test the therapist in transference terms, according to Weiss (1971), Sampson (1976), Silberschatz (1978), and Weiss and Sampson (1986) (who are all part of the San Francisco Psychotherapy Research Group). These studies suggest that patients follow an "unconscious plan" that affects how and when the patient may test the therapist's response through an issue in the treatment relationship.

During and after such "tests," it is important for the therapist to try not to be drawn in to the negative roles that may be set off by the patient's behavior but, rather, to remain as neutral as possible. In that way, the therapist is doing his part not to repeat the disappointing or traumatizing behavior the patient is likely to have experienced with earlier "objects." This can help the patient recognize the role of the transference, as illustrated by the following example from the treatment of Mr. Peter Quinn:

EXAMPLE: Mr. Peter Quinn

In these excerpts from successive sessions, the therapist responds by pointing out that the patient is testing the relationship with the therapist for its fit with the CCRT's version. These tests dovetail with the central relationship theme, which is at the heart of the transference problem (more fully discussed with the CCRT in Luborsky, 1997).

P: I heard the details of the good job you [the therapist] did in handling the staff problem in your department. I must tell you.

T: You want to see whether in our relationship we can tolerate your saying to me that I am adequate.

[Next session]

P: I thought over what I heard about the job you did with the staff problem in your department. I don't see it was much of a contribution. It really was just common sense.

T: You want to see whether we can tolerate your wish to put me down and to try to make me feel inadequate.

Principle 6: Repair Ruptures in the Helping Alliance to Further the Treatment

When the therapist senses that a problem has developed in the Helping Alliance such that the patient and therapist are no longer effectively working together, a cycle of *rupture and repair* can get the treatment back on track. Rupture and repair refers to a process through which the patient and therapist examine the problem event together, along with the therapist's open acknowledgment of any real elements in the difficulty, so as to move back toward an alliance in which the patient can feel understood.

EXAMPLE: Ms. Michelle Young

The patient is typically engaged and animated during sessions. But for the last two sessions, she has become increasingly cool and reserved. In this session, after about 10 minutes, she stops and shrugs.

P: Nothing else to say.

T: That is interesting. You usually have a lot to say, but today it's different.

P: [Shrugs and smiles slightly] Guess so.

P: I wonder if something happened here that could have made you feel differently.

P: [Says nothing and sits in silence for a few minutes]

T: Let's see, I might have said something. . . .

P: Or did?

T: OK, let's see what I did.

P: Well, I know this sounds trivial, but I don't really like when people yawn. . . .

T: No wonder you're not talking! When did I yawn?

When the therapist brought up the possible link between his own behavior and the patient's, that facilitated the patient's bringing up a perceived slight. After talking over the real behavior and its implications, the therapist acknowledged that he had been tired, but not tired of the patient. From there the patient was able to talk about her own feelings with renewed involvement.

Safran, Muran, Samstag, and Stevens (2001) reviewed the empirical research on rupture and repair. They found that while the field of study is still in its early stages, there is evidence for the association of a rupture and repair process with a positive outcome of treatment for some patients, particularly those who tend toward negative reactions in relationships.

PRINCIPLES OF RESPONDING: WORKING WITH THE PATIENT IN TREATMENT

Principle 7: Make the Core Conflictual Relationship Theme the Shared Focus of the Treatment

After the patient's CCRT has been discovered, detecting its emergence in the patient's symptoms and life can become a shared focus. Each time the CCRT emerges, the patient and therapist can reach greater familiarity with its workings. The therapist can refer to the shared search by saying "We can now see . . . " after they have revisited the CCRT pattern in a different form. The use of the word *we* amplifies the shared process, which is useful for the Helping Alliance, as well as for the advances of the expressive work for Ms. Harding:

EXAMPLE: Ms. Vicki Harding

The patient began treatment because she was in a state of chronic mild depression. She noticed her friends moving on with their lives, but hers was at a standstill. In the same job for 10 years and the same apartment for even longer, the patient was bored with her familiar routine but did nothing to change it.

P: I can't tell you how many nights I've spent home watching Jay Leno.

T: Must be getting monotonous.

P: That's an understatement. Boring is more like it. Boring and depressing, and I see people around me having lives. The woman in the next apartment just had a baby.

T: It must feel lonely to see others moving on and be at a standstill yourself.

P: [Nods]

T: Wonder what we can do to help you get unstuck.

P: [Shrugs]

After more efforts to forge an alliance around that theme, the patient was roused out of her dysthymic state and came to terms with her fear that if she made any changes she would be all by herself.

P: Which, of course is what I am now—all alone, I mean.

The patient then began to get curious about why she'd been stuck so long. The therapist helped the patient identify the "self response" (RS) of giving up as fundamental to her CCRT pattern. The patient then revealed early frightening experiences, which seemed to make sense in light of her very strong tendencies to keep anything at all new from happening. The therapist's active efforts at alliance building helped the patient feel supported enough to engage in an exploration of a core theme and its origins, which started a process of "baby steps" toward change.

Principle 8: Tailor the Level of Understanding to the Treatment Needs of the Patient

Patients differ considerably in how much insight into their core conflict they need in order to change, as well as in how long it takes to achieve that meaningful understanding. While some patients are able to make use of a rather brief period of delving into the relationship problems in order to make a change, others need a much longer, more involved process.

Some patients can benefit considerably from small changes in certain areas of functioning (Brenman, 1952; Schafer, 1991), while others make no change at all under similar circumstances. As described in the chapter on supportive relationships (chapter 9), some patients need a prolonged period of empathy and alliance with the therapist in order to begin the expressive work. Keeping alert to individual differences helps the therapist tailor the treatment to each patient's needs.

Principle 9: Attune Responses to the Patient's Central Message

The process might be called the *matching-of-messages test*. It works by comparing the patient's central message with that of the therapist's main responses.

The review can be done by the therapist, from her recollections, along with the assistance of some process notes. A reasonable match between the patient's and therapist's messages indicates a successful session. The first research study on the matching of messages (Auerbach & Luborsky, 1968) found moderately significant agreement between three judges in rating this variable. The procedure followed by each judge in that study was to specify the patient's main communications, then to specify the therapist's main responses. The scales for this method can be found in appendix C.

More recent research on the same topic has relied on the CCRT as a measure of the patient's main communication (Crits-Christoph, Cooper, & Luborsky, 1988, 1990; Crits-Christoph & Luborsky, 1988). The comparison of the patient's CCRT with the themes in the therapist's interventions makes for a reliable measure of accuracy of the interpretations. This is a useful approach for determining the accuracy of interventions, one that has clinical and research applications.

Principle 10: Examine the Functions of Defenses

Many of the CCRT responses of self may serve the function of a psychological defense. For example, a patient may respond to perceived or expected criticism from others by habitually withdrawing from social situations. In this case, the patient is protecting himself from anticipated harm by withdrawing. Understanding the reason for the behavior provides a way to help the patient gain some awareness of its quasi-automatic functioning. After noticing the sequence of behavior, the therapist might say, "Well, if it turns out that you are right, and everybody *is* going to criticize you, no wonder you wouldn't want to go anywhere new."

Perry (1993) defines a defense as "an individual's automatic psychological response to internal or external stressors or emotional conflict" (p. 277). Defenses typically constrict or distort the patient's responses. Common defenses include avoidance, denial, projection, and dissociation. Noting their workings as they become evident in the treatment can help in untangling the "self" element of the CCRT.

Principle 11: Keep Interpretative Statements Simple

Responses should not be overcomplex, either in length or in content. In fact, it is a good practice for the therapist to divide responses so that he can be guided by the patient's response to each part. When too much material is presented all at once, the patient may have trouble absorbing it. Complex or lengthy interpretations can backfire by diffusing the patient's attention and disrupting her train of thought. It is always useful to bear in mind that the treatment is foremost a place *for the patient to speak.*

Principle 12: Develop Patience with the Patient's Process and Progress

The therapist needs patience to keep the treatment process essentially the patient's. The therapist must not only avoid overloading the treatment with interpretations but must also keep from responding for the sake of making a response. Ironically, the therapist's desire to cure the patient can get in the way of giving the patient the time to tell his story and discover the sources of the central problems. Learning to listen and to deepen the listening is an effective way to counter the therapist's own need for progress. This counteracts the tendency to jump in too quickly.

Such patience sets a model for the patient, who can learn to reflect and to appreciate silence through the therapist's stance. When the therapist does not offer immediate interpretations or solutions, it can convey trust in the patient's abilities to come up with material and answers himself.

Fewer therapist interpretations keep a session as an occasion for the patient's self-expression. In fact, some evidence suggests that infrequent interpretations may be prudent—Connolly and colleagues (1999) discovered that the usual number of interpretations in the early sessions of SE psychotherapy is low, only two per session; the study concludes that it is best kept low. Piper, Joyce, McCallum, and Azim (1993) also found that the accuracy of interpretations had an impact on outcome, but their quantity did not.

Principle 13: Time the Responses to the Patient in Relation to the Time Span of the Session

The beginning of the session is a good time to listen afresh to what the patient brings. For this reason, it is useful to wait for 5 or 10 minutes after a session starts before responding. The middle phase of the session (the next 20 to 30 minutes) is the best time for the therapist's actual responding to take place. In contrast, the end phase of the session (the last 5 to 10 minutes) is the time to draw the session to a close rather than to introduce new ideas or material that might need to be processed.

Principle 14: Turn Countertransference into a Source of Information

Countertransference responses are an inevitable part of the process of psychotherapy. While some forms of countertransference suggest problems in the treatment, others provide valuable information about the patient and the treatment. The therapist may be able to deal more effectively with countertransference if she has an understanding of its different forms (Singer & Luborsky, 1977). Five different types are described here.

Type 1: Personal countertransference responses are the counterpart of the patient's transference responses. They have to do with reactions, or issues of the therapist's, that are triggered by either the patient or the material being discussed. A good way to protect against having this type of response is through self-understanding. The therapist's personal psychotherapy is recommended for that purpose. In that way the therapist will have awareness of his own issues and can use that awareness to screen for personal countertransference reactions.

Type 2: Immediate responsiveness, without taking the time to think over what the patient has said, typically takes place when the therapist has become overinvolved in the topic. This tends to cause the therapist to lose the distance needed to stay with the patient's central theme. *Open listening* can help counteract this tendency by putting the therapist into a frame of mind where he can take his time to understand what the patient is intending to say.

Type 3: Shared affect states grow through the nonverbal transmission of strong feeling states. They can be used productively to give the patient a sense that the therapist understands the patient's feelings, or they can cause the therapist to "lose his balance" as therapist.

A *contagion of moods* (a term suggested by Redl, 1966) refers to the transmission of affect states—experiences without modulation or subsequent reflection. For example, if the patient is depressed, the therapist "catches" the depression; if the patient is happy, the therapist becomes happy. When the patient is most caught up in relationship problems, the patient is likely to be experiencing the most stress. If the therapist experiences that stress at the same level as the patient, he will not be as helpful to the patient as he might otherwise be.

However, if the therapist does not share the patient's affect state at all, he will be "tone deaf" to the feel of the patient's experience. Shared feeling states can be a valuable way for the therapist to key into the patient's emotional life. They offer a prime source for empathy and can help the therapist respond to the patient's pain and pleasure—just as in early life a parent uses attunement (Stern, 1985) as a way to respond to an infant's affect states. Shared affect states can be forms of connection with patients in treatment, as in the early attachment (Luborsky, 1999; Fonagy, 2001). Problems with such states occur if there is a loss of boundaries and the state becomes the therapist's actual mood state, rather than a quasi-state, used to help further the treatment.

Greenblatt (1959) has illustrated the mutuality of emotional responding through parallel psychophysiological recordings of the patient and therapist. If the therapist monitors his own affect state and is aware of this form of affective resonance, it can keep him from "catching" the patient's mood (Butler & Rice, 1963). Awareness also allows the therapist to make use of the forms of understanding that may come through affective channels.

Whether the therapist is *field independent* or *field dependent* has an effect on the process of affect transmission. Witkin (personal communication, 1970; Witkin, Lewis, & Weil, 1968) found that extremely field-dependent therapists are more likely to get caught up in *emotional contagion*. However, highly field-independent therapists are likely to stay so uninvolved that they would not be able to form a warm relationship with the patient. Therapists who are moderately field dependent could well be the most able to form a positive Helping Alliance (Luborsky, Crits-Christoph, Alexander, Margolis, & Cohen, 1983).

Type 4: A specific countertransference response, called *negative interpersonal fit*, may occur when the therapist behaves in ways that fit into the patient's negative expectations. Such a negative fit turns out to be more common than has been supposed (Singer & Luborsky, 1977). For example, a therapist found that he could never remember the appointment time of one particular patient. He then realized that this experience dovetailed with the patient's frequent experience that "everybody passes me over; nobody pays me any mind."

If the therapist's response does fall into a *negative fit*, the honest acknowledgment of the problem can turn the problem into a treatment opportunity. The therapist needs to get herself ready to be both tactful and nondefensive so that the patient has the chance to react to what is probably a frequent experience. At its best, this allows the lapse into a negative fit to become an experience where the patient is able to examine the interpersonal workings of an aspect of his relationship problem.

Type 5: Countertransference can at times provide *information*, offering clues that inform the therapist by providing an active sense of what the patient is experiencing. In that way, the countertransference can have positive value for the therapist's understanding.

Such information may come through the therapist's awareness of otherwise puzzling reactions to a particular patient. For example, a therapist found himself always becoming sleepy within the first few minutes of the session with a young woman he was treating. In self-monitoring, the therapist wondered whether he was sleepy for other reasons. That turned out not to be the case; he was always quite alert for the patients before and after this woman. He then began to wonder if he found the patient boring for some reason. He came to the conclusion that the patient did present herself as dull. The therapist hypothesized that she was "putting him to sleep" as a way to put to sleep whatever disturbing material the patient was warding off. He was able to use this insight to "wake up" the patient, the treatment, and himself.

Principle 15: Make Use of Inclinations to Respond Countertherapeutically through "Near Responding"

Sometimes the therapist may experience an inclination to respond countertherapeutically. This would naturally feel like a major interference. After all, his intention is to establish a positive Helping Alliance and to try to like the patient. But he will find some patients less easy to like than others and will sometimes struggle not to have a negative reaction to the attitudes or behavior of a particular patient.

Rather than simply pushing away such reactions, it can be beneficial to pay attention to them. It can be useful to discuss them with a colleague or supervisor or find a way to fully understand any personal reactions that the patient's behavior sets off in the therapist. It is also important to consider how the behavior could be a communication to the therapist. This principle follows directly from the section on countertransference since it deals with the therapist's uses of his reactions to the patient.

EXAMPLE: Mr. Carter Franklin

The patient had just spent his fifth session detailing the renovations in his country house, berating the workmen, and talking about his accumulating wealth. Was he trying to put himself above the therapist, or did it only seem so to the therapist, who did not share the patient's good fortune in finance. The therapist was trying not to react, but he couldn't help but feel put down, at least by implication. He sought the consultation of a colleague, who offered to review the understanding of the patient to see if they could better interpret the patient's communication that way.

The patient had entered treatment because he felt like an imposter in the world of "big shots." Everyone around him was successful, and he just "talked the talk." His father had always berated him for being a slacker at school and not becoming a successful athlete. He set out to prove his father wrong and was on his way toward his first million . . . except he was haunted by nightmares and had a fractious relationship with his wife, who had insisted he "get help."

So here he was, where he didn't necessarily want to be, in therapy, having to admit he had a problem. "Having a problem" could mean his father was right, the supervisor theorized. Maybe putting the therapist down was a way to pull himself up so that his father's predictions could be false. The therapist came to the conclusion that it would be useful to talk over how the patient felt about being in treatment. He anticipated that it could move into a discussion of his feelings toward the therapist and his own self-esteem, which it did eventually do.

Principle 16: Notice Changes toward Positive Ways of Responding from the Patient

At any point in the treatment, but especially in its later phase, the patient may begin to offer more positive responses to situations that used to cause conflicts. With some patients, this may take the form of a clearer vision of what the patient would like for himself. For other patients, it may take the form of greater ease with themselves or a reduction in anxiety. Noticing this growth is an important part of helping the patient hold on to the gains. The value of noting the positive is consistent with Seligman's views on the desirability of emphasizing positive qualities for personality growth and health (Seligman & Csikszentmihalyi, 2000).

Some patients are fearful of improving because it could mean that the therapist will no longer be interested in them. This is sometimes an unexpressed fear, since getting better begins to imply needing to give up the help of the therapist. Talking over any such concerns about getting better can clear the room for going forward.

LISTENING AGAIN

Once the therapist has responded to the patient, she returns to listening. In this phase of listening again, the therapist combines the *open listening* stance of phase 1 with all that has happened between the patient and the therapist in the session. The therapist may reflect on the shared understanding of the session so far while attending to the patient's statements and reactions. The patient's reactions and responses lead the way toward what comes next.

While the therapist continues to keep the patient's CCRT in mind as she listens, the directions that they move toward will come from the patient. The therapist will naturally hear that material in relation to the accumulating CCRT understanding so that his next responses can integrate where the patient and therapist have been with where they are now.

Since the patient knows what he needs to convey, the therapist cannot script the session. Rather, he can continue to stay open to where the patient goes. Knowledge of the principles of listening and responding helps the therapist develop an ability to fluidly move back and forth between current material and past material, using both the Helping Alliance and the CCRT as anchors in the process.

Listening again after responding puts the session back where it belongs—with the patient. The therapist's role is to facilitate a gradual process of self-awareness that can lead to change.

SUMMARY AND DISCUSSION

This chapter discusses the therapist's expressive task: to follow through with the main steps in the therapeutic process of *listening*, *understanding*, *responding*, and *listening again*. In order to respond to the patient, the therapist must balance the need to stay in tune with the patient with the need to advance the understanding of the patient's central problem. While each patient brings his or her own unfolding patterns to the treatment, the therapist paces his responding to develop a way to work together that fits each patient.

The therapeutic response can be guided by the recurrent use of the fundamental expressive response principles given in this chapter, including linking the symptoms with the CCRT components, working through the CCRT, and focusing on the relationship with the therapist. The previous chapter describes how the therapist listens to the patient through *open listening* and listens for the components of the patient's CCRT pattern. The present chapter is an overall guide to the content of the therapist's response, which often includes the components of the CCRT, as well as some of the sources of difficulty and their resolution.

The guide for responding described here may sound easy on paper, but it requires much practice to carry out effectively. It means attending to the flow of expressed thoughts on a main topic within a session or across sessions by using the SE principles. It also means translating what is said into an understanding of the workings of the CCRT in a way that can be heard by the patient.

Chapter Twelve

The Closing Phase of SE Psychotherapy

"How will you know when I'm done?"

Patients frequently ask this question early in treatment. In the midst of the turmoil that has brought the patient into treatment, there may be doubt that the problems and symptoms can ever be resolved, or a lack of understanding of what could make things change. The therapist might say, "We will both know when you are done. It will be when the problems that brought you in are not in your way anymore." In other words, the therapist can let the patient know that the treatment will be finished when the broader goals have been achieved. In time-limited SE psychotherapy, the same concerns may exist about whether the patient could actually "be done" or "get better," but the time limit answers the question in practical terms.

The question comes up all over again when the closing phase in SE psychotherapy may in fact be near. It may also come up when there is trouble in the treatment. Keeping track of the goals of the treatment can help to discriminate a "false end" from a real one, while keeping an eye on the CCRT can guide the sense of how much mastery the patient has achieved over problematic patterns. In the end, greater well-being and more positive approaches to life will optimally replace the symptoms and negative states that brought the patient into treatment.

Studies of the CCRT indicate that in a successful SE treatment, the patient's wishes tend to remain much the same, but the expectations from others (RO) and of self (RS) undergo change (Luborsky, 1998). In other words, by the end of treatment the patient tends to be less negative in his expectations and less "in his own way."

Patients in SE psychotherapy differ in how "done" they need to feel before ending treatment, so an open hearing of the patient's thoughts about ending can facilitate reaching a comfortable decision. While the therapist may have a sense of how much he hopes the patient will gain from the treatment, in the end the decision rests with the patient, just as it did when the patient decided to begin.

PREMATURE TERMINATION

Sometimes the patient feels pressure to terminate the treatment quickly. It is useful to determine the source of the pressure in order to work with the patient's best interest in mind.

Sometimes the pressure comes from outside of the treatment, either from a significant other or from problems with finances or an insurance plan. At other times the pressure comes from the patient himself, either because of dissatisfaction with the treatment or because of a problem he has encountered in the treatment relationship.

It is useful to determine if the pressure is due to a change in a real dimension of the patient's world (such as a financial problem) or to a therapeutic impasse. Taking the issue seriously is the first step, with an inquiry into the problem's sources. Pressures from others in the patient's life may be due to their emotional reactions to the patient's treatment (such as jealousy), or they may be a way for the patient to represent her own concerns in an indirect way. Again, an open inquiry into the problem is a necessary first step.

Treatment impasses are often due to reactions to events in the therapeutic relationship, as described in the previous chapter. This may include an actual event, along with a reaction that is part of the patient's CCRT. A sequence of rupture and repair may benefit the treatment at this juncture. The therapist will want to stay open to seeing the issue through the patient's eyes.

ENDING THE TREATMENT

Once the decision has been reached to end the treatment, a set number of final sessions needs to be established so the patient and therapist have time to review the core themes and deal with any remaining issues. In addition, the therapist will want to note the achievements of the treatment, with specific attention to any changes in the negative elements of the CCRT pattern. In that way, the therapist is working to help the patient hold onto the gains.

Symptoms may recur during this phase, but the patient should have more awareness of their meanings and should be able to resolve them much more quickly than in the early phases of treatment. There is a world of difference between a symptom that comes "out of the blue" or a relationship pattern that "keeps happening" and those same problems once the patient has a handle on their meanings and functions.

ENDING THE THERAPEUTIC RELATIONSHIP

Ending the therapeutic relationship itself is an important topic for the closing phase in SE psychotherapy, in both time-limited and open-ended treatments. If a patient does not bring up that topic during the termination process, it is an important one for the therapist to raise, since concerns about leaving the therapist can disrupt the termination. Working with those concerns provides a final phase to consolidate the gains that come through a positive Helping Alliance. The therapist will want to help the patient find ways to hold onto the feelings of support associated with the Helping Alliance, while moving through anxieties about ending.

Patients in any psychotherapy often ask about the possibility of calling or being in touch with the therapist in the future. As with the question of whether this is a "real" time to end, the therapist needs to discriminate between unfinished therapeutic goals and a natural wish to keep in touch. Once the patient and therapist have established that this is a real and realistic ending time, the therapist can offer an "open door." This policy has the symbolic function of keeping the therapist in mind as someone who is always potentially available to the patient. It also may have a real function should the patient find the need for treatment in the future.

EXAMPLE: Ms. Sarah Satin

P: I think I'm done. . . . What do you think?

T: Let's hear your thoughts about that.

P: When I started coming in here, my life was a complete mess. I couldn't make any decisions, and everything seemed overwhelming. [Looks at T, who nods] But it's not like that now. I mean I got a job that I actually like, and I have some decent friends, not the kind that tell you what to do and dump on you. [Laughs]

T: And you have your own ability now, to make choices that you are happy about.

P: I'm glad you said that. I was afraid you'd disagree or raise your eyebrows, and then I would know I was all wrong.

T: Who does that?

P: My mother, I know. . . . And I also know you are not her. How about that?

T: [Smiles]

P: So what happens if I fall apart and I can't deal with anything as soon as I walk out the door?

T: Sounds as if it is scary to think about ending, even though you have made enough progress here to feel ready to do it.

P: Yeah. Can I have your card?

T: [Gives patient a card, just as he did at the beginning of treatment]

This card means that the therapist will be there after they finish working together, just as the first card meant that he would be there while they worked through the patient's core problems.

While this patient was able to bring up the possibility that she would "fall apart" after termination, some patients act out that fear through a brief recurrence of symptoms during the termination phase. The behavior needs to be discussed in relation to the patient's fears and CCRT reactions. If the behavior does not remit during the time allotted for ending, the therapist will need to evaluate whether this is a transient reaction or a sign that the termination is premature. In the end, the overall best interest of the patient should be the guide, rather than a termination date.

CRITERIA FOR COMPLETION OF SE PSYCHOTHERAPY

The criteria for the completion of treatment depend on whether it has been a predominantly supportive or a predominantly expressive therapy, as well as on the initial Health-Sickness level of the patient. When the treatment has been predominantly supportive, the criteria for being ready to end therapy have to do with improvement in the patient's functioning and symptoms. The therapist can consider termination if the patient now has other supports in her life and has reached a stable period.

In a successful expressive treatment, the patient should have gained some insight into his problems and mastery over his core themes. If the patient has been working toward positive solutions to his symptoms and CCRT patterns during the final phase of treatment, that helps his readiness. Those gains should help him in his future responses to situations that trigger his core themes.

Here is an example of a patient interviewed 8 years after treatment using the RAP (the relationship anecdotes paradigm) interview method—the RAP is an interview method in which the patient or subject is asked to recall an anecdote about a relationship event (Luborsky, 1990).

EXAMPLE: Mr. Edward Howard, during a RAP interview at an 8-year follow-up (Luborsky & Crits-Christoph, 1998).

During the RAP interview, the patient described an event that took place with his supervisor at work:

During his evaluation, he thought the supervisor, who grew up in Hungary, told him, "You're a loaf" (meaning to the patient "you are a loafer"). The patient admitted that this activated his worst fear, "that I would be seen as an ineffectual do-nothing." But he then reflected on his reaction and "worked hard to counteract this image that I had of myself" (p. 119). It was then that he figured out the supervisor was actually saying, "You are *aloof*," that some people think you don't care.

For this episode, three independent judges summarized the scores they gave for the interview, rating this as an experience of "rejection" or "criticism," and it was followed by feeling frustrated and angry. The inferred wish was "to be close and cared for by the other person." When the other person rejects or criticizes, he becomes frustrated and angry and in such a context is likely to become symptom-prone. The important aspect of this example is that although he was still vulnerable to the core theme, he was able on his own to make a correction of his "perception" of a rejection.

In the closing phase of SE and SE session-limited psychotherapy, many gains should be evident. Optimally, they include mastery over the presenting problem, both in real-life terms and in terms of a better understanding of the CCRT pattern. The mastery should be such that it changes the automatic nature of the negative CCRT pattern. In spite of these gains, it is often rediscovered that the person is still vulnerable to the original symptom. In those situations, the person tends to have more insight into his vulnerabilities, as in the previous example, and can make his own preparatory corrections for them.

SUMMARY AND DISCUSSION

All psychotherapies need a way to come to an end, one that helps the patient feel ready to hold onto what he or she has learned in the process. SE and SE session-limited both use the CCRT as a way to come to terms with the problematic patterns behind the patient's problems. In the closing phase of SE, those themes should be reviewed in language that stays with the patient's understanding of the problem. In treatments that have been primarily supportive, the emphasis is on a greater sense of well-being and functioning rather than on insight.

Regardless of how supportive or how expressive the treatment, the Helping Alliance has been a central tool in moving the treatment forward. For that reason, the therapist's confidence in the patient and her gains, as well as her acceptance of remaining anxieties or concerns, helps the patient hold onto the gains.

In all terminations, but perhaps especially in session-limited treatment, a review of the patient's new ways of coping can be helpful. At times when the gains seem shaky, the therapist can let the patient know that further treatment in the future is always an option. Sometimes anxiety over ending treatment can make a patient seem less able to cope than he really is. In the end, the patient's gains are his to take out the door.

PART IV

COMBINING AND COMPARING SE PSYCHOTHERAPY WITH OTHER TREATMENTS

Chapter Thirteen

Combining Medication with SE Psychotherapy

Whether to add medication to a patient's psychotherapy is a question that arises with increasing frequency. It is an issue that may be brought up by the therapist or by the patient. This is due in part to advances in psychopharmacology, making more forms of psychoactive medication available. It is also linked to an increased awareness and acceptance of the use of medication, along with a rise in the biological views of symptoms.

Along with these changes come opportunities and potential risks. The combination of medication with SE psychotherapy can be helpful when the patient seems unlikely to benefit adequately from psychotherapy alone, or after a trial of psychotherapy has revealed more serious symptoms. The nature and severity of the patient's problems are pivotal in that consideration. This is particularly true when the seriousness of the symptoms warrants an active approach to recovery, as in a major depression with suicidal risk.

But sometimes the use of medication can be offered as a substitute for resolving inner conflict or for overcoming interfering CCRT patterns. In an era where pills are advertised as solutions to many problems, it is useful to consider the different treatment options and their possible consequences. Relying on medication alone to resolve symptoms overlooks the opportunity to understand and defuse the symptom through the Symptom-Context method. But combining medication with psychotherapy can be beneficial for some patients.

Principle 1: Treatments Combining Psychotherapy with Medications Tend to Be More Effective for Some Patients than Psychotherapy Alone

Much comparative psychotherapy research has shown that adding pharmacological agents to psychotherapy can assist the progress of *some* patients

(Klerman et al., 1994). Knowledge in this field expands from year to year, as reviewed by Luborsky, Mintz, et al. (1980). In a later review by Luborsky, Crits-Christoph, et al. (1988) of 15 studies, 12 showed a significant advantage for a combination treatment; 3 of these studies showed a nonsignificant difference. Most of these studies used dynamic psychotherapy, of which SE is a principal form, according to the descriptions in the studies (Docherty, Marder, Van Kammen, & Siris, 1977). These studies tended to be weighted toward inpatients, especially schizophrenic patients, although other studies of combination treatments, including those with neurotic outpatients, showed similar trends. However, a more recent large-scale study comparing combination treatment with psychotherapy alone found no advantage in combination treatment for patients with mild depression. (Thase et al., 1997).

Principle 2: The Nature and Severity of the Patient's Condition Affects the Outcome

The next sample is a very large one—595 depressed patients in six treatment protocols (Thase et al., 1997). All patients met the criteria for unipolar, nonpsychotic, primary major depressive disorder. They were given 16 weeks of either cognitive-behavioral therapy or interpersonal psychotherapy alone, with or without medications. Meta-analysis revealed that in mild depressions, combination therapy was not significantly more effective than psychotherapy alone, but a very significant advantage was observed in more severe recurrent depression.

This study also gave new evidence in support of the conclusion that the combination treatment—of medication and psychotherapy—is superior to psychotherapy alone in the treatment of severe recurrent depression. However, since the combination did not give greater benefit for patients with mild depression than psychotherapy alone, this result supports the importance of considering the nature and severity of the problem when thinking of adding medication.

Are these treatment combinations beneficial either as an *additive* effect or as a *mutual facilitation* effect? In a review by Smith, Glass, and Miller (1980), combined treatments were found to produce a treatment effect size that was larger than either treatment's effect size alone; yet, *the combination turns out to be largely additive rather than mutually facilitative*. A similar result was found in four studies of tricyclic antidepressants in combination with psychotherapy as compared with either treatment alone or with no treatment. An additive effect was shown for the treatment of unipolar moderately depressed patients (Weissman, 1979).

Principle 3: Taking Medication May Have Both Positive and Negative Effects on the Psychotherapy

Medications may have a variety of positive and negative effects on the psychotherapy, as summarized in Klerman et al. (1994). Here are some of the possible positive effects: the medications may facilitate accessibility, they may have positive effects on patients' expectations, they may facilitate compliance and adherence, and they may have a rehabilitation effect. Of these four, the last one, the rehabilitation effect, is the prime reason to consider their use.

Taking medication may instead have negative effects: The patient may see himself as "sicker" or as having a mental illness, the reduction of symptoms may incorrectly imply to some patients that psychotherapy can be discontinued, the patient may devalue the therapist in contrast to the psychiatrist or psychopharmacologist, and the medication may undercut commitment or motivation in psychotherapy.

The therapist is the one in a position to have a balanced view of the treatment. It is useful for the therapist to examine her own reactions to considering medication for the patient. Sometimes, a therapist may discover that she is invested in keeping the treatment "pure" and therefore wishes to avoid medication. Or, she could find that the appeal of medication is in part to diminish the strain of working with an interpersonally difficult patient. Examining her own reactions can help the therapist become ready to work from a position of the "best interest of the patient."

The therapist will want to explore with the patient the meanings of taking medication so that it does not have an untoward effect. With some patients, the combined treatment is a simple, straightforward arrangement that allows for relief from unmanageable levels of pain. With others, it brings meanings, as described already, that may affect the patient's motivation or views of the treatment. In those cases, it becomes a treatment issue to untangle. In order for it to be a helpful combination, it is optimal for the patient and therapist to monitor its different kinds of effects.

Principle 4: Psychotherapists Who Are Not Qualified in Psychopharmacology Should Collaborate with a Medication Expert

When psychotherapists are not trained in the uses of psychotropic medications, or are not able legally to prescribe them, they should consult with an expert, such as a psychiatrist or a psychopharmacologist. It is useful for the therapist to gain information about possible side effects of the prescribed medication. The physician will need to meet with the patient at regular intervals in order to monitor the medication response and the patient status.

While some psychiatrists prescribe medication along with doing psychotherapy, another practice is to have one practitioner handling medication and another providing psychotherapy. In inpatient settings, it is common practice to assign each patient both a psychiatrist and a psychotherapist, with the psychiatrist prescribing the medications as well as making management decisions. In outpatient practice, it is also common to seek out an expert to evaluate and prescribe medication. However, some therapists may choose to treat only those patients who are not in need of medication.

Principle 5: The Therapist Should Learn What Taking Medication Means to Each Patient

Inevitably, taking medication has a special meaning for each patient. One source of meaning has to do with the therapist and the therapy itself. The therapist should explore the meanings each patient gives to taking medication (Group for the Advancement of Psychiatry, 1975; Docherty et al., 1977).

Many of the meanings may tie in with the patient's CCRT pattern. Some of the usual meanings include believing that taking medication shows a lack of self-control, assuming that taking medication means that the psychotherapy is useless, thinking that the medication is the effective part of the treatment, seeing the therapist as less able than the psychopharmacologist, or seeing the therapist as powerful for arranging for the medications.

Each patient brings his or her own reactions to the situation. When these reactions are linked to the patient's CCRT pattern, working with this instance of the pattern helps unify the treatment.

Principle 6: The Patient Should Understand the Expected Effects of the Medication

The patient has a right to know what the medication is given for, as well as any side effects that might occur. Having a clear sense of the purpose of a medication can help diminish possible misinterpretation. The prescribing doctor will typically review such information, but it is useful for the therapist to understand it as well. Some of the most common uses are to treat the symptoms of anxiety and depression, as well as the serious mood fluctuations of a bipolar disorder. If a patient has suicidal tendencies, antidepressant medication can be vital for stabilizing the patient.

Principle 7: Medication Should Not Be a Substitute for Dealing with a Relationship Problem between the Patient and Therapist

It is all too easy to turn to medication when a patient becomes more symptomatic. However, the therapist needs to consider the possible meanings of the symptom. For example, does it occur in the context of a CCRT theme in the relationship with the therapist? If so, that should be examined before considering adding medication. This consideration is worthy of exploration, since medication could cover up the relationship problem by giving symptom relief and diminishing the need to look further.

CONDUCTING RESEARCH ON PSYCHOTHERAPY AND MEDICATION

In psychotherapy research studies on the uses of psychotropic medication, there are various options on how to schedule their use. One option is to start all patients on medication at the same time. While this method gives temporal consistency, it does not take into account that different subjects are likely to be at different levels of need for the medication.

Another option used by the Penn Psychotherapy Project (Luborsky, Mintz, et al., 1980) is to prescribe medication to patients at the time they are in greatest need. The desired results from this *open-ended* option follow: The groups being compared probably will get what they need in terms of medications, but the groups compared probably will not have different amounts of prescribed medications by the end of treatment. Also, if the groups do get different amounts prescribed, the amounts will not correlate with the main variables of the study (i.e., will not be enough to correct for differences in the groups).

In the Penn Psychotherapy Project (described in Luborsky, Mintz, et al., 1980), the use versus nonuse of medications did not have a significant relationship to the outcome measures. Of the 73 patients, 36% were prescribed some medications during the course of the treatment. These prescribed medications were small to moderate doses of ataractics (antianxiety medications) such as chlordiazepoxide hydrochloride and diazepam, or antidepressants such as amitriptyline hydrochloride (Elavil).

Another study (DeJonghe, Kool, Van Aalst, Dekker, & Peen, 2001) compared the cost-effectiveness of a combination of clomipramine and dynamic psychotherapy with clomipramine alone for patients with major depression. The 74 subjects, age 20 to 65, were given 10 weeks of treatment for major depression. Improvement was substantial in both groups. Combined treatment patients had less in-treatment failures and better work adjustment at the end, with a cost savings of $2,311 dollars per subject.

DeJonghe et al. (2001) compared the efficacy of antidepressants alone with that of antidepressants plus psychotherapy in the treatment of depression. The antidepressant sample size was 34, and the combined therapy sample was 83. Of those subjects who had 16 sessions of psychodynamic supportive psychotherapy, much like the SE psychotherapy, 32% refused pharmacotherapy;

13% refused combined treatment. Combined treatment was significantly more successful than pharmacological treatment alone: At 24 weeks, the success rate was 40.7% in the pharmacotherapy alone group and 59.2% in the combined therapy group.

A major gain in the treatment benefits of psychotherapy for drug addiction is found through combined treatment (e.g., the use of naltrexone with the BRENDA behavioral procedure) (Volpicelli et al. 2001), which was better than "talk" therapy alone. It was effective in the majority of alcohol-dependent patients.

SUMMARY AND DISCUSSION

The combination of psychotherapy with medication has considerable evidence to support it, especially with severe and recurrent disorders. The evidence is not so clear for less severe problems, notably for mild depression (Thase et al., 1997.) It is important to find the best combination for the particular patient (Klerman et al., 1994).

The calling in of a medication expert is recommended, unless the therapist is also trained to prescribe such medication. (Two states already have legal support for psychologists to take on this role). Even then, some prefer a "split treatment," in which one person does the psychotherapy and another prescribes the medication. Every department of psychiatry where training is done has some practitioners with this knowledge; some of these people may be called in to consult. It is helpful to find a consultant who is knowledgeable about combining psychotherapy and pharmacotherapy (Kay & Gabbard, 2003).

The use of psychotropic medication with and without psychotherapy has increased considerably in the past two decades. It also has become better recognized that research helps guide information about which diagnostic groups benefit most from medication and combined treatments.

It is now common for patients to raise the question of whether they should take medication. Because of this, it is useful for the therapist to be informed about the current uses of different types of medication. However, being informed does not mean the therapist should assume that his knowledge is accurate or complete. The therapist's role is to make a determination about whether the addition of medication would be likely to benefit the patient. Having the patient consult with an expert is necessary to confirm the decision, as well as to determine the specific choice of medication.

Chapter Fourteen

Comparing and Combining Psychotherapies

SE is one of several commonly practiced forms of psychotherapy, which are often compared with each other. Sometimes aspects of the different treatments are combined with each other as well. In order to better understand these trends and their implications, a brief review of the common psychotherapies is included here.

In doing SE psychotherapy, adjuncts to the treatment are sometimes beneficial, notably forms of family treatment and the uses of patient evaluation. These practices are discussed here as well.

The different clinical topics to be considered in this chapter include the following:

- *The common psychotherapies:* This section begins with an account of the most frequently cited forms of psychotherapies; it is necessary to have adequate descriptions of each form of treatment in order to consider the literature on comparing and combining psychotherapies.
- *The family and similar therapies:* It is sometimes helpful as an adjunct to both SE and SE session-limited psychotherapy to include people who are close to the patient in the treatment or to refer them to another therapist.
- *The probable effects of managed care organizations on the treatment:* When psychotherapies are carried out with the involvement of a managed care organization, there are often problems for the psychotherapist to watch out for.
- *Diagnostic evaluations of physical health:* A physical examination should be routinely recommended to the patient before the start of psychotherapy.
- *Diagnostic evaluations of mental health:* Sometimes a diagnostic psychological examination should be recommended as well, especially where cognitive deficits are likely or need to be ruled out.

THE COMMON PSYCHOTHERAPIES

There are actually hundreds of similar but differently labeled psychotherapies, but we will describe those most commonly performed in the Western world, including the United States, Canada, England, Europe, Israel, Australia, New Zealand, and even the Far East. These forms of psychotherapy are also the ones for which professional training is most often given, at least for psychiatrists, psychologists, and social workers. For each of these common psychotherapies, we give the gist of the treatments, including the types of patients for whom they were designed and research about their possible benefits.

1. *Supportive psychotherapies:* Supportiveness is a treatment quality that is present to some degree in all psychotherapies. It is an important component of SE and SE time-limited, as described in chapter 9. But treatment whose main techniques are supportive is well suited to the treatment of more seriously ill patients, as indicated both by their Health-Sickness level and their diagnosis. Two research comparisons of long-term supportive treatment with psychoanalysis showed that both treatments benefited patients—one showed that their impacts probably did not usually differ significantly (Wallerstein, 1986; Blatt & Zuroff, 1992); a third study showed that more introjective (self-critical) patients did better with psychoanalysis (Blatt & Felsen, 1993).
2. *Expressive psychotherapies:* All of the dynamic types of psychotherapies, including the supportive-expressive ones, have some of their origins in psychoanalysis. These dynamic psychotherapies share a belief in the importance of free expression, while the therapist and the treatment usually also provide supportive conditions.

   As described throughout this book, supportive-expressive psychotherapy is a form of dynamic psychotherapy that uses the CCRT to guide the treatment and the conditions for the treatment. It includes both the SE open-ended form and the SE session-limited form. This form of therapy can be utilized with a broad range of patients because of the relatively easy alteration of the proportions of supportiveness and expressiveness. It is also well researched—there have been about 70 studies of SE and of SE session-limited (Hilsenroth, Ackerman, Blaggs, Balty, & Money, 2003).
3. *Cognitive-behavioral psychotherapy:* Cognitive-behavioral psychotherapy (CBT) has contributed much to clinical practice as well as to psychotherapy research (Beck, Rush, Shaw, & Emery, 1979). The typical time-limited treatment length, as in SE session-limited psychotherapy, is short, with a usual range of about 12 to 20 sessions. In the past approxi-

mately 40 years, CBT has been aided in its development by an enlarging cadre of practitioners and researchers.

The explicit focus of the psychotherapy is on finding and then correcting the patient's maladaptive patterns of thinking. The therapist helps the patient identify the precise content of the "faulty thinking" and then teaches a variety of cognitive and behavioral methods to challenge and modify the distorted thinking. Between sessions, the patient is given cognitive or behavioral homework assignments; the homework assignments reinforce the therapeutic methods by which patients can modify their own maladaptive thinking and behavior. Cognitive-behavioral psychotherapy originated as a treatment for depression, but it has been applied to a wide range of psychiatric disorders.

4. *Behavioral psychotherapies:* This set of treatments has a long historical lineage. At its core it builds on the behavioral theories of John B. Watson (1913), Ivan Pavlov (1927), and Joseph Wolpe (1969), who hold that the causes of symptoms are generally to be found in faulty mental associations. The "psychotherapy" at its start was a literal outgrowth of Pavlov's well-known study involving the sounding of a bell each time a dog salivated in response to presentation of food—the "unconditioned stimulus." Then, with repetition, the bell alone became the "conditioned stimulus" and even by itself would be associated with salivation. The task of the behavior therapist is to find the stimulus for the symptoms and repair the faulty associations on which they are based. Currently this approach is most often used with phobias.

COMPARISONS OF DIFFERENT TYPES OF PSYCHOTHERAPIES WITH EACH OTHER

In the field of treatment comparisons, there has been a "hot" conflict going for the past few decades—between those who believe there are major differences between empirically supported treatments and those who believe there are few important differences. Clinical research tends to support the latter point of view. Following are some of the bases for the conclusion: The *research* literature offers much support for the conclusion that there is a tendency for a nonsignificant difference effect for outcomes when any of these psychotherapies are compared with each other (Luborsky, Rosenthal, et al., 2002; Luborsky, 2001; Luborsky, Singer, & Luborsky, 1975; Luborsky, Diguer, Seligman, et al., 1999). Comparisons among different treatments tend to be small, and when corrected for differences in researcher allegiance, they are even smaller (Luborsky, Diguer, Seligman, et al., 1999). In a recent study

(Luborsky, Barrett, et al., in preparation), the difference for 17 meta-analyses of psychotherapy outcomes with different types of treatments was only about .10 (by Pearson correlation), which is quite a small difference.

One of the common *clinical* conclusions is that a more supportive psychotherapy is likely to be a good match to more severely ill patients. While that is a reasonable overall conclusion, even here there are exceptions. One school of opinion believes, for example, that Kernberg's (1975, 1984) treatment approach for borderline patients is most suitable for that patient group, even those who are severely ill—and there is some support for that view. However, more research on the benefits of supportive treatment with more seriously ill patients would be useful.

While these clinical and research trends will probably receive more support in the next few years, for now there is no consistent evidence that any one type of treatment is superior to the others. Recommendations for clarifying the differences include making sure that researchers have different allegiances from each other and that both researchers and clinicians have a high degree of familiarity and experience with the treatments being compared (Luborsky, Barrett, et al., in preparation).

In spite of the lack of findings, the movement toward empirically supported treatments continues, with the assumption that research supports only certain forms of treatment for specific disorders. Westen, Novotny, and Thompson-Brenner (2004) suggest shifting away from efforts to validate "treatment packages" toward looking for ways to offer "empirically informed therapies." That would include taking into account the empirical evidence for the factors in psychotherapy that have been linked to positive outcome, such as the Helping Alliance, along with seeking a better understanding of the "g," or general factor, in effective psychotherapy.

THE INFLUENCE OF LENGTH OF TREATMENT ON THE OUTCOME OF TREATMENT

Orlinsky, Grawe, and Parks (1994) examined the findings to date on the duration of treatment. Out of 156 findings, 100 (or 64%) found a positive link between the length of treatment and outcome. "Overall, the findings indicate that patients tend to improve more the longer they stay in treatment" (p. 352).

An important study on the value of length in psychotherapy was conducted by Blomberg, Lazar, and Sandell (2001). It compared the effectiveness of long-term psychoanalysis with long-term psychotherapy. The average duration in this study was 40 months for the psychotherapies and 51 months for the psychoanalyses. Patients completed questionnaires, including the Symptom

Checklist (Derogatis, Lipman, Covi, Rickels, & Ublenhuth, 1970), the Sense of Coherence Scale, and the Social Adjustment Scale. There tended to be small to moderate effect sizes for psychoanalytic psychotherapy, versus moderate to very large effect sizes for psychoanalysis. During treatment, the proportion of patients with more healthy scores increased from 10% to 75% in the psychoanalysis group and from 30% to 55% in the psychotherapy group. The psychotherapy group was equated as closely as possible with the long-term psychoanalytic group in terms of the levels at the beginning, middle, and end.

The main comparisons of these psychodynamic treatments show a fair amount of agreement between long-term psychoanalysis and long-term psychotherapy on these measures. For both treatment groups, there is a significant linear trend across time, showing that *both* long-term psychoanalytic psychotherapy and long-term psychoanalysis are helpful. But, the before-treatment to late-after-treatment increase was 61% in the psychoanalytic group and 25% in the psychoanalytic psychotherapy group, which means that the psychoanalytic group improved more with time than the psychoanalytic psychotherapy group (Blomberg et al., figure 5, p. 376).

In this comparison, a likely principle may be that "more is more," meaning that the psychoanalytic group had a more intensive, longer treatment. However, new research on this question would be helpful, including allegiance effects in the study of the benefits of forms of longer treatment.

SIGNIFICANT OTHERS JOINING THE TREATMENT

SE psychotherapy typically is an individual form of psychotherapy, but this does not mean that it must always be restricted in its application to the patient alone. The patient may have problems with family or family-like relationships that could benefit from some joint sessions with one or more of these people: parents, siblings, spouse, or other partners. The sessions with an additional person or persons provides a chance to understand the views of the significant others in the patient's life.

Before making any change in the form of the treatment, the therapist needs to leave room for the patient to air fears or fantasies about its possible impact on the therapeutic relationship. Even if the change is brief or temporary, it is useful to keep a shared awareness of any concerns it awakens in the patient.

Here are some gains from adding significant others to the treatment:

1. The patient and therapist can use the joint session to better understand the patient's problems in a relationship by witnessing them together. The understanding may be deepened by noticing parallels between the relationships

with those "others" and any tendencies toward similar forms of interaction with the therapist.

2. Sometimes other members of the group can form a treatment bond around helping the patient and can then be enlisted by the therapist as therapeutic change agents. This is most likely to occur if the patient has an illness that needs family support, or in the case of a child or adolescent who needs family understanding.
3. Another way to focus the therapeutic work is on beneficially changing the group structure. This approach has been artfully presented by Minuchin (1974), who works with the family as a whole and sees the problem as rooted in the "family system" rather than in the patient alone. For some patients, there is enormous relief at no longer being seen as "the sick one" or "the black sheep" in a family full of problems.
4. Often it is the patient's idea to bring in a family member in order to get help with a problem in a current relationship. It can be helpful to discuss with the patient how it might feel to bring in this person, even if it is the patient's idea to do so. Similarly, it is necessary to explore the motives behind the idea before going ahead. Sometimes the patient's wish is for the therapist to "fix" a difficult family member; sometimes it is for the therapist to see more fully how impossible that person is. If it does turn out that both patient and therapist feel it is in the patient's best interest to bring in the significant other or others, then the patient can extend an invitation to join a session or series of sessions.

EXAMPLE: Ms. Andrea Martin

After about a year and a half of therapy, Ms. Martin expressed an interest in having her husband join her in some psychotherapy sessions because "I'm afraid we'll never get anywhere with this [a sexual problem]. And he won't go to therapy himself. But I asked him if he would come with me, and he said 'OK' to that."

During the next 6 weeks, the patient continued her weekly sessions, but her husband joined her for an additional session. The patient was able to use the presence of the therapist to speak more openly about her hopes to "have a love life again." The therapist supported the husband in moving through his embarrassment about talking through his side of the problem. The patient was relieved by this additional intervention and felt it was unlikely that they would have "gotten anywhere" without it.

Work with the couple or other family members is often better handled by referring the patient to another therapist for that aspect of the work (e.g., as a form of family therapy or individual treatment for another family member). This is the case when the "group issues" would be likely to take the focus away from what is central to the patient in his own treatment, or if it would be problematic for the patient to "share" the therapist. The therapist needs to consider the potential impact on the Helping Alliance before including others in the treatment.

SPECIAL PROBLEMS OF DOING PSYCHOTHERAPY IN MANAGED CARE SETTINGS

Starting in the 1980s, managed care organizations began to grow in influence, as discussed in the brief history of this movement by Kihlstrom and Kihlstrom (1998). The managed care organizations tend to be of two kinds: (1) a group practice that employs psychotherapists among its other practitioners and (2) a management and referral system that offers cases to practitioners in their network. Both of these types of organizations tend to be run as businesses, where many decisions are based on the contribution of each activity to the "bottom line" (i.e., to the net amount of money the organization generates by providing psychotherapy and related services).

A major limitation in working with a managed care organization is that it has the right to make decisions that may affect patient care, although the organization could hardly have the best interest of the patient as its main criterion. Another limitation is the necessity to provide clinical information to the insurance companies, following the categories set by the industry.

If psychotherapy is provided by managed care organizations, it is typically brief—often between 6 and 20 sessions. The control on the provision of extra sessions by the managed care company typically follows guidelines that appear to be primarily aimed at reducing the expense of the treatment. With the large expansion of managed health care companies, much psychotherapy is now done through such organizations.

When the patient seen under these conditions raises a concern about the treatment limits, it can be useful for the therapist to discuss the issue with the patient in such patient-centered terms as "*We* should discuss this together to figure out what *you* wish to do." When the managed care company will not authorize more sessions, although the patient and the therapist believe they are needed, one alternative is for the patient to pay for the treatment and therefore no longer have to depend on the managed care company. This is possible if the patient is able to afford the fee himself or if the therapist is able to reduce her fee for the patient.

When therapists work within these structures, it is useful to accept the reality that the managed care company typically does limit the length of the treatment. The recommendations for doing SE session-limited psychotherapy in chapter 3 should prove instructive under these conditions.

RECOMMENDED PHYSICAL EXAMINATIONS

Since medical problems sometimes masquerade as psychological problems, it is always valuable for a patient to have a good medical examination when beginning treatment. A thyroid condition, for example, can cause a depressed mood. It is also possible that a psychological problem interacts with physical health, as in the case of the link between negative moods and worsening cardiac conditions (Carels et al., 2003).

As a precautionary measure or for specific physical questions, a physical examination helps establish a baseline of health for all patients when they are about to start or have just started psychotherapy. The example of Mr. Adam Berger illustrates the general and specific value of the physical examination.

EXAMPLE: Mr. Adam Berger

The patient had been experiencing impotence for over a year, which he feared meant that he had contracted a sexually transmitted disease—"something terrible," he concluded. It took many weeks of encouragement and exploration of his fears for Mr. Berger to make an appointment with his doctor. He was immensely relieved to discover that he did not have any sexually transmitted diseases, nor did he appear to have any physical cause for his impotence. That allowed him to explore his guilt over his extramarital affairs in the therapy, with a gradual realization that he might be "stopping himself from doing it."

RECOMMENDED PSYCHOLOGICAL EXAMINATIONS

Psychological examinations are often recommended to measure clarity of thinking and intellectual functioning, as in the following example of Mr. Nathan Perry. This kind of assessment is not always necessary, yet in some cases it can reveal valuable information that informs decisions about the particular type of treatment needed.

EXAMPLE: Mr. Nathan Perry

Mr. Perry had frequent memory lapses and was concerned that they might mean he had "something truly wrong with my brain." Both a physical evaluation and a neuropsychological assessment were performed, which indicated that his memory lapses were not evidence of brain disease. The information was a relief to the patient and permitted more attention to the psychological sources.

INTEGRATION OF TREATMENTS

Integrating forms of treatment is increasingly frequent, as illustrated through the rise in the number of therapists who consider themselves "eclectic" in their theoretical orientation. As noted already, combined treatments sometimes include the addition of family or couples therapy to individual treatment. It may at times also mean the addition of a specific technique that has been found to be helpful for a specific problem, such as relaxation or breathing techniques for anxiety disorders. Wachtel (1993), for example, describes integrating behavioral techniques with dynamic treatments.

Consideration of the integration of treatments with each other also comes from the question of how to move beyond the "Dodo bird finding," described in chapter 1, that while psychotherapy does show benefits, no one form has been shown to have ownership on those gains. That research has served as an impetus for the development of clinical thinking on psychotherapy integration (Greenberg, 2002).

In fact, recent research suggests that therapists of all orientations tend to use intervention strategies that may fit with the patient at hand. Thompson-Brenner and Westen (described in Westen et al., 2004) measured the intervention strategies of psychotherapists. They found that psychodynamic therapists reported using more CBT interventions (e.g., structuring the therapy hour) with emotionally constricted patients, while CBT therapists reported using more psychodynamic interventions (e.g., exploring patterns in relationships and unconscious processes) with emotionally dysregulated patients. This suggests that therapists may make adjustments in the treatment that end up making the different orientations less different.

However, research suggests a note of caution about combining treatments. In Orlinksy, Grawe, and Park's (1994) comprehensive research on outcome, links were found between outcome and how skillfully the therapist goes about his role. Two important aspects of the therapist's skill were maintaining a stable frame and adhering to a treatment model. This could mean that combination treatments run the risk of losing the integrity of one treatment model.

It may be that the two findings are not as contradictory as they might first sound. The earlier finding could suggest that therapists tend to make adjustments for pathology without necessarily changing the treatment frame. However, this consideration needs to be followed up by further research inquiry.

SUMMARY AND DISCUSSION

This chapter reviews common forms of psychotherapy, along with research comparing these different forms. Research consistently finds nonsignificant differences between treatments, referred to as the Dodo bird finding. The question of how to "move beyond the Dodo bird" is discussed, with recommendations about attending to researcher allegiance and continuing to look into the "g," or general factors, contributing to effective psychotherapy.

Ways to add forms of treatment that may complement SE psychotherapy are described, notably forms of family therapy. The uses of diagnostic evaluations of physical and mental health as adjuncts to SE or SE session-limited therapy are also reviewed. Finally, the integration of treatments is considered, with the finding that therapists tend to make adjustments within treatments to fit with the clinical needs of the patient, which may make for less difference between treatments in reality than in theory.

PART V

SUMMARIES: LINKING RESEARCH AND PSYCHOTHERAPY

Chapter Fifteen

The Steps in SE Psychotherapy: A Review

"Why is it that we have two ears and only one mouth?"
"Because it was meant that we should listen twice as much as we should speak."

The core of the therapist's role in SE psychotherapy is expressed through this dialogue from the Talmud between a young rabbi and his senior rabbi. The therapist's most fundamental task is to listen to the patient; the rest of the treatment flows from there.

These are the basic steps of the treatment process:

1. *Listen to the patient.* Listen to what the patient has to say about herself and her core problems. Listen for the sources of pain, for repeating themes, and for hopes. Open listening is a skill the therapist cannot do without. It forms the basis both of his alliance with the patient and of his understanding.
2. *Prepare the patient for SE psychotherapy.* Many patients find it easier to become active participants in the treatment if they understand how it works. In some settings, such as a clinic, this can be done through an "anticipatory socialization interview" (Luborsky, 1984) by a member of the staff. In other settings, such as in private practice, the therapist can explain the fundamentals of the treatment process during the early sessions. The patient can be encouraged to "say what comes to mind" so that the sources of his problems will gradually emerge. In SE session-limited psychotherapy, the patient needs to be clear about the frame of the treatment from the beginning.
3. *Make treatment arrangements clear.* During the first session, the therapist needs to make clear the main arrangements for (1) the length and frequency of the sessions, (2) the fee, (3) the policy for missed appointments,

(4) the time when termination might be considered, and (5) whether the treatment will be SE or SE time-limited.

4. *Help the patient decide on treatment goals.* During the first session or two, the therapist should help the patient articulate his main goals for psychotherapy. This should be rediscussed from time to time in order to help keep the goals in mind. In addition, it provides a chance to change or modify the goals, particularly when the treatment is not time limited.
5. *Forge a positive Helping Alliance.* In the early sessions, it is essential to establish the sense of working together with the patient, either as a team effort (Helping Alliance, type 2) or with the patient feeling that the therapist is someone who will be able to help (Helping Alliance, type 1). Over time, the state of the Helping Alliance may need the therapist's attention in order to keep the treatment on track.
6. *Decide on the balance of supportiveness and expressiveness.* Determine the balance of supportiveness (chapter 9) versus expressiveness (chapters 10 and 11) that the patient's treatment is likely to need. This is achieved through early assessment of the patient, as well as through trial efforts at establishing the right approach for the patient. Patients with fundamental disturbances in reality contact or functioning need more reality-focused support, while many other kinds of patients can benefit from more expressive work.
7. *Figure out whether to add medication.* Decide whether medication might be helpful in addition to the psychotherapy by considering whether the patient's symptoms are serious enough to warrant it. Both the degree to which the symptoms may be dangerous to the patient and the likelihood that they could be resolved by psychotherapy alone go into such considerations. Those issues need to be discussed with the patient and with a medication consultant, as needed.
8. *Formulate the main theme of the CCRT.* Formulating the CCRT pattern is the essence of the expressive work. In the early sessions, the therapist will listen for its elements, until the whole pattern gradually comes into view. The main theme of the CCRT will emerge in different spheres of the patient's life and guide the therapist's interventions.
9. *Decode symptoms through their context.* The context of symptoms provides clues to understanding their meaning. If the therapist helps the patient become curious about the links, then they can engage in a shared process of making sense of symptoms through the Symptom-Context method.
10. *"Work through" the understanding.* Keep in mind that the treatment is called "a process" because the patient needs to understand her life in a new way. It takes time and repeated incidents that can be understood and

reunderstood for the patient to "work through" how the CCRT pattern appears in her symptoms and life.

11. *Attend to the meanings of termination.* Well before termination arrives, it is necessary to begin to prepare for it. That includes reviewing the understanding of the core problems and patterns and working through what it means to the patient to end the treatment. The main purpose of this process is to consolidate the gains of the therapy so as to help the patient maintain the gains after the treatment itself is over.

Chapter Sixteen

Twenty New Ideas for Clinical Research

Psychotherapy itself is a prime source for investigating the treatment process as well as the formation of symptoms (Luborsky, 1992). A few research ideas will be summarized here as a springboard for future work. We have no intention of being encyclopedic. Rather, we intend to offer suggestions about promising areas to investigate that we and others may explore in our next studies, as well as a few ideas that could lead to new research topics.

One promising area concerns the connection between psychological and neurological processes. Researchers now have the tools to begin exploring the relationships between them, due to the expansion of methods in both fields. These advances increase the potential to understand the connection between spheres that had once been considered dichotomous; an example of that effort comes through the study of the neurological underpinnings of the CCRT pattern (see chapter 4).

Another important area of research continues to be the source of the effectiveness of psychotherapy; our frequent findings of nonsignificant differences in the global effectiveness of psychotherapies can be followed up in different ways. One is through more research on the common factors in psychotherapies. That means continuing to look for what is essential in treatment, apart from tradition, ideology, and therapist allegiance.

Efficacy research, done through research studies, needs to continue being compared with the "effectiveness" (Seligman, 1995) of clinical work in natural settings. This recommendation is relevant to evidence-based practice, for which a wide range and complexity of patients and their problems need to be studied.

Here, then, are 20 good ideas and techniques as principles for research, offered as help for planning psychotherapy research.

RESEARCH IDEAS CONNECTED WITH THE CORE CONFLICTUAL RELATIONSHIP THEME (CCRT) METHOD

1. The Neurological Pathways to the CCRT

The underlying brain location activated by the CCRT has been identified through functional magnetic resonance imaging (fMRI; Loughead et al., in preparation). This finding should be followed up with more research into the neurological underpinnings of CCRT activity. Our hope is to come closer to an understanding of the neurological concomitants of the CCRT.

2. The CCRT and Attachment Patterns

Both attachment patterns and the CCRT find enduring ways of dealing with relationships with others and responses from the self (Ainsworth, Blehar, Waters, & Wall, 1978; Main, Kaplan & Cassidy, 1985). A study of CCRT patterns in young children's narratives (Luborsky, Luborsky, et al., 1996), which has yet to be followed by further studies, suggests an overlap between the two systems. Adult attachment patterns (Brennan, Clark, & Shaver, 1998) could well be correlated with certain kinds of CCRT patterns. More exploration of the relationship between the CCRT and attachment patterns has the potential to enrich the understanding of both.

3. CCRT Responses of Self and Defense Mechanisms

As discussed in chapter 11, the CCRT "responses of self" could be an operational version of what are referred to as "defense mechanisms" (Perry, 1993). Following up on this hypothesis could lead to fruitful study of the "self" mechanisms and their possible groupings. Empirical research on how defenses function could be furthered by such an investigation.

4. An Improved Set of Variables in the Standard Category List

One of the ways to score the CCRT is to use the lists of standard categories of wishes, responses from others, and responses of the self (Luborsky & Crits-Christoph, 1998). Continuing to improve the lists of categories facilitates using them in comparisons with other systems.

An improved list of variables should allow for more rapid scoring and be more encompassing than the spaces of a "grid." A comparison of the grid with other forms of recording is now in development; it suggests that the original version of the standard categories is not sufficiently broad as is the one by Albani et al. (2002). While the current system is adequate in terms of reliability, there is room for more development in this area.

IDEAS FOR NEW USES OF THE SYMPTOM-CONTEXT METHOD

5. The Conditions for the Appearance of Anxiety

Symptoms of anxiety, in its various forms, are relatively common. Because they are increasingly treated with medication, patients may miss the opportunity to link the symptom with the trigger. Research using the Symptom-Context method could enhance the understanding of anxiety formation through its links to its context (Luborsky, 1996). This method of studying anxiety has the potential to improve understanding of forms of anxiety and their treatment.

6. The Symptoms Associated with Post-Traumatic Stress Disorder (PTSD)

The Symptom-Context method offers a way to understand symptoms of post-traumatic stress disorder (PTSD) as they appear in psychotherapy and in the patient's life (see chapter 5). Symptoms of PTSD are typically intense and disruptive and often take somatic forms. Patients are helped when they can link their symptoms to their meanings, especially in relation to their past trauma. The Symptom-Context method can be used to study these interconnections, thus furthering the understanding of the symptoms and the routes to treatment. These could be combined with the fMRI studies in order to view the interaction of the Symptom-Context with neurological functioning in PTSD.

7. Stress-Related Medical Conditions

The Symptom-Context method offers a way to help patients "get a handle" on the specific forms of stress that might set off stress-related medical conditions (see chapter 5). There is potential to carry that further, as both a clinical and research tool. Considerable room exists for study of person-specific and syndrome-specific emotional stressors and their links to physical health.

IDEAS TO INCREASE THE THERAPIST'S CONTRIBUTION TO OUTCOME

8. The Therapist's Effects on Outcome

The testing of therapist effects on outcome is important, but it has received little attention so far. In psychotherapy practice, the qualities and experience of the therapist carry weight. But some researchers have suggested that the variation among therapists contributes only a small percentage, such as 3% to 5%, to the explanation of treatment outcomes (Crits-Christoph et al., 1991). Further research will be helpful in clarifying which kinds of "therapist effects" make a difference.

9. Consistency of Therapist Performance

Another way to look at the therapist's contribution is to consider how consistently therapists achieve certain outcomes. It appears to be true that therapists who perform well in one study also tend to perform well in other studies (Luborsky, Diguer, McLellan, Woody, & Seligman, 1997).

Consistency of the therapist's performance could be further examined through looking at treatment outcome and patient complaints. This approach may offer a way to revalidate the clinical impression that the quality and the experience of the therapist do matter.

10. A Method of Studying Countertransference

Countertransference has attracted more positive clinical interest in recent years. While previously considered a pitfall of treatment, it is increasingly looked to for its potential contributions to the therapy (see chapter 11).

While efforts to study countertransference have begun (Butler, Flasher, & Strupp, 1993), it remains a vital topic in need of a method. If a method of studying countertransference can be constructed, then its effects on treatment can be more effectively evaluated.

11. Accuracy of Interpretation

Piper, Joyce, McCallum, and Azim (1993) found that while *frequency* of interpretations did not affect outcome, *accuracy* of interpretations did. The accuracy of interpretation has been examined by Crits-Christoph, Cooper, and Luborsky (1998), by means of moderate to good reliability and validity studies. More studies would be beneficial to give further backing to this area of research.

MORE DEVELOPMENT OF CLINICAL RESEARCH METHODS

12. A Comparison of Results for an Aggregate Analysis versus a Detailed Within-Case Analysis

The aggregate method of combining cases for analysis is the usual method in clinical research. However, within-case analysis, as can be done with the

Symptom-Context method, offers data that more closely resembles the psychotherapy process. This form of analysis shows promise in its ability to do fine-tuned psychotherapy research, but the method needs more development.

Comparisons between these two kinds of studies would be beneficial. It may turn out that each method has a contribution to make, and we should determine how much overlap they have.

13. "Sudden Gains" and Their Potential in Treatment Research

Sudden gains are defined as those that appear suddenly and are at least one standard deviation or more above the average gain in benefits. These gains are measured by the Beck Depression Inventory applied to the text of the psychotherapy sessions. Tang, Luborsky, and Andrusyna (2002) used the measure of sudden gains during a session as a way to compare treatments. Cognitive-behavioral therapy and supportive-expressive (SE) psychotherapy showed considerable similarity in relation to sudden gains, although a few differences were detected.

The Health-Sickness Rating Scale (HSRS) (Luborsky, 1962), whose background and definition are given in chapter 6, has been consistently successful in predicting outcome. In a recent study, the correlation between Health-Sickness and outcome of treatment was about .60 for a sample of 17 cases (Luborsky, Stuart, et al., 2001). The sudden gains measure should be applied after the Health-Sickness level of the patient is taken into account.

14. More Study of the Role of the Length of Treatment

Significant questions remain in the study of the effects of treatment length. Length in itself may be only a modest factor, but there is some evidence that it leads to better outcome (Luborsky, 2001). When patients had the option to continue treatment as long as needed, the outcome was improved. This finding not only supports the role of length as a variable affecting the treatment but also suggests the advisability of studying the role of the patient's choice as well.

More studies are necessary before a conclusion about the relative effectiveness of short-term versus long-term psychotherapy can be supported. In brief, comparisons between long-term versus short-term treatment have frequently yielded nonsignificant differences. However, none of the treatments were actually long; "long term" in many of those comparisons is only long term by comparison with the short-term treatments studied.

In studies of long-term treatment, longer term is associated with better outcome. Orlinksy, Grawe, and Parks (1994) found that patients tend to improve more the longer they stay in treatment. More study is needed to better understand how length of treatment may contribute to outcome.

MORE WAYS TO STUDY THE EFFECTIVENESS OF PSYCHOTHERAPY

15. Comparisons of the Effectiveness of Types of Psychotherapy

We recently surveyed 17 meta-analyses comparing types of psychotherapies with each other (Luborsky, Rosenthal, et al., 2002). While the Dodo bird conclusion still stands in this review, larger collections of comparative data will help further the field of treatment research.

In spite of many studies in this area, questions remain about whether differences among treatments are meaningful in relation to outcome. If there are generally nonsignificant differences in the outcome of treatments, are there nevertheless different qualities that are transmitted by different kinds of treatments? In other words, do all roads lead to Rome, or do they lead to other cities as well?

As described elsewhere, the search for evidence-based therapies has recently dominated the dialogue on this topic, in spite of methodological concerns, notably about the generalizability of the findings. This increases the need for more sound studies in this area.

16. More Examination of the Effects of Combining Treatments

While the clinical trend is toward more eclectic forms of treatment, research suggests that it is beneficial for the therapist to maintain adherence to a treatment model (Orlinksy, Grawe, & Parks, 1994). Are there forms of integration that are successful, while others lose the focus of the work?

Therapists have been found to modify the treatment in response to patient characteristics (Westen, Novotny, & Thompson-Brenner, 2004). This may be a different phenomenon, one of a therapist's adapting to the needs of patients. However, this is a topic in need of closer examination.

17. Consideration of the Researcher's Allegiance and the Therapist's Competence in Studies of Psychotherapy

Recent research on researchers' allegiance and on therapists' competence indicates that they both play a major role in comparisons of psychotherapies (see Luborsky, Diguer, Seligman, et al., 1999). Luborsky, Barrett, and colleagues (in preparation) offer a number of recommendations to improve psychotherapy research that emerge from these findings. Basic to those recommendations is to assess allegiance of the judges prior to any comparative treatment study and to use a sample of therapists who have a high degree of competence in doing the form of psychotherapy being studied. Attending to the competence level of the therapist and the allegiance of the researcher will improve the validity of comparative treatment studies.

18. More Study of the Central Curative Factors

The study of factors that are central to all psychotherapies is a subject worth more examination. One way to understand the Dodo bird finding is that the central factors may be of greater importance than the variations among treatments. The Helping Alliance is an example of one of the central factors consistently found to be linked to positive outcome (Miller, Luborsky, Barber, & Docherty, 1993).

Another way to further clinical research would be to focus on how the central factors may combine; combined factors may have different effects than the factors separately. Here are some factors that should be examined for the ways they might work together: (1) mastery (Grenyer, 2002), (2) Helping Alliance, (3) credibility—a judgment by a clinician that a treatment is likely to be effective (Berman & Luborsky, in preparation), (4) HSRS, (5) length of treatment, and (6) frequency of mentioning people (Mitchell, 1995)—a method that requires a count of each person the patient mentions.

19. Follow-Up on Major Qualities Drawn from the Psychotherapy Research

Variables that have been found to have links with effective psychotherapy can give clues for continued study. In the Penn Psychotherapy Project pilot study, Luborsky, Crits-Christoph, Mintz, and Auerbach (1988) examined which dimensions of treatment affected outcome. Out of the factors studied, the two that reached significance were the therapist's "ideal relationship," which refers to the therapist's warmth and unconditional regard, and the patient's involvement. Although these two qualities can be subsumed by a positive Helping Alliance, their specific impact could nonetheless be further explored.

Orlinsky, Grawe, and Parks (1994) reviewed the process and outcome literature to date. They found these factors to be consistently linked to outcome:

1. The overall quality of the therapeutic relationship
2. The therapist's skill
3. The patient's openness versus defensiveness
4. Treatment duration

Including these dimensions in future studies could help researchers further understand what really matters in psychotherapy and could help clinicians do "empirically informed" treatment.

20. The Newest Idea

Each clinical experience is an opportunity for hunches to be followed up with meaningful clinical research. The newest idea has yet to emerge.

SUMMARY AND DISCUSSION

These 20 research ideas are offered as suggestions of the areas that might pay off in discoveries. Two of these ideas seem especially promising:

1. *The connections between psychological and neurological processes:* Researchers now have the tools to begin exploring the relationship between these two spheres, thanks to the expansion of methods in both fields. An example of that effort as shown in chapter 4 comes through the study of the neurologic underpinnings of the CCRT.
2. *The sources of the effectiveness of psychotherapy:* Our frequent finding of nonsignificant differences in the *global* effectiveness of psychotherapies can be followed up in different ways. One is through more research on the common factors in psychotherapies. That means continuing to look for what is essential in treatment, apart from tradition, ideology, and therapist allegiance.

Chapter Seventeen

The Interplay of Clinical Hunches with Research Discoveries

There is no better launching ground for new psychotherapy research than hunches derived from doing clinical work. A clinical *hunch* emerges when different forms of understanding are synthesized rather than added together. Clinical principles sometimes grow out of such hunches, but they can also serve as an impetus for research studies. They may be used as a basis for hypotheses about clinical processes, as well as to develop methods of investigation that are sensitive to clinical work. Translating clinical concepts into the language of research is probably the hardest part of the task.

Since psychotherapy and research use different languages of inquiry and require different training, there is typically a gap between the two. They are often considered as two separate enterprises with different values. The frequent problem that researchers have with clinical principles is that they are too "soft" to be tested precisely; the frequent problem that clinicians have with research is that the methods are "reductionistic" and do not preserve the richness of the clinical process.

These concerns have been increased by a focus on evidence-based practice, which compares defined "treatment packages" through methods of study that are appropriate for some forms of treatment but not for others (Westen, Novotny, & Thompson-Brenner, 2004; Luborsky & Barrett, in press). Yet research and psychotherapy *can enrich each other* if they forge a path that respects both forms of inquiry.

The interplay of clinical experiences with research investigation makes for the beginnings of meaningful clinical research. Without such an interplay, there is a risk that the research does not correspond sufficiently to the forms of inquiry that are intrinsic to clinical work. If it cuts out all material that is nonexperimental, then little of the value is left (Doss, 2004).

DISCOVERING CLINICAL RESEARCH METHODS

In the past 40 years, I have worked to develop research methods that grow out of clinical understanding, most notably these four: the Core Conflictual Relationship Theme method (CCRT) (chapter 4), the Symptom-Context method (chapter 5), the Health-Sickness Rating Scale method (chapter 6), and the Helping Alliance methods (chapter 7).

These research methods give a scientific dimension to fundamental clinical concepts. They each began with a construct that is crucial in dynamic psychotherapy. By taking a careful look at procedures that underlie those concepts, it became possible to translate them into measures that retain their clinical essence. They illustrate the interaction between the two levels: the level of clinical concepts and the level of operational research methods.

The Core Conflictual Relationship Theme Method

The idea of a central relationship pattern has a long history; it was a concept in need of a method. While the analysis of the transference has a valued place in psychodynamic circles, it has been regarded with suspicion in other places because it lacked scientific validation.

That was mulling around in my mind when I reheard the voice of a resident I trained (Perry Berman), asking for more clarity about the transference and how it was to be inferred. I recognized the truth in his question. That prompted my paying close attention to exactly what went into the formulation of a transference pattern. I realized that clarity could benefit not only clinical training but also the study of the central relationship pattern itself.

The Symptom-Context Method

I worked with my early mentor Raymond Cattell on a method he was developing for doing valid research on data within an individual, through what he called "P-technique." Around the same time, Freud's clinical studies on daydreams and slips of the tongue were in the back of my mind. Freud's clinical method of understanding phenomena by their context was described in that work.

That helped set the context for this method. There had to be a way to study how symptoms form in an individual patient. Why not use the psychotherapy session as a source for the data, using "within an individual" data, as Cattell had?

The idea seemed like a natural fit, one that could help research progress. One should be able to identify the meanings of the symptoms more readily when their context is known. After developing the method and then applying it to a series of cases, I wrote a book about the method, appropriately called *The Symptom-Context Method* (Luborsky, 1996).

The Health-Sickness Rating Scale Method

The Health-Sickness Rating Scale method began as a group effort at the Menninger Foundation. We noticed that clinicians typically began case reports with a description of the level of illness of the patient, suggesting that they used the description as a baseline for their impressions of the patient.

There was potential for a method that could help clarify a dimension we suspected was important in predicting treatment outcome. In most studies at that time, the clinical-quantitative view of the background had been insufficiently represented. The HSRS solved that need. Eventually this was recognized by others, most evident in the adaptation of the HSRS to become Axis V in the *DSM-IV*.

The Helping Alliance Methods

While working on the Penn Psychotherapy Project, starting in 1976, I became impressed once again by the importance of an alliance with the patient, quite apart from the CCRT pattern. The Helping Alliance is a clinical concept that had taken many forms, but it had yet to have a form that could be measured. Without a way to measure it, the contribution of the Helping Alliance was all too easy to overlook.

Just as I had anticipated, its measurement has played a part in confirming its importance in understanding psychotherapy outcome. Different forms of numerical measures make it possible to determine whether the patient, the therapist, and an independent observer see the Helping Alliance in the same way. These methods give the therapeutic relationship different ways to be included in psychotherapy research.

THE VITAL LINK: A SUMMARY

We have reviewed the origins of four clinical research methods: the Core Conflictual Relationship Theme, the Symptom-Context method, the Health-Sickness Rating Scale method, and the Helping Alliance method. Each illustrates how clinical and research thinking can benefit each other.

Research findings can enrich clinical practice not only by giving it credibility but also by adding to the therapist's tools and understanding, as the

CCRT and the Symptom-Context method have done. These methods have already influenced practice and given rise to new research findings. Readers are invited to find further uses for the methods described in this book, as well as to develop new ones. In that way, the vital link between research and practice can continue to grow and evolve.

Appendix A

CCRT Scoring: Standard Categories

Thought Unit (1-5 Scale) Ratings

Standard CCRT Categories
WISHES
Date: ______
Rated by: ______
(Write in the thought unit →
Rate it and note P or N)

Edition 3 (clusters)	Edition 2					
1. To assert self and be independent	21. To have self-control					
	28. To be my own person					
	34. To assert myself					
	23. To be independent					
2. To oppose, hurt, and control others	18. To oppose others					
	16. To hurt others					
	19. To have control of others					
3. To be controlled, hurt, and not responsible	15. To be hurt					
	20. To be controlled by others					
	29. To *not* be responsible/obligated					
	13. To be helped					
	27. To be like others					

4. To be distant and avoid conflicts	17. To avoid conflicts					
	14. To not be hurt					
	10. To be distant from others					
5. To be close and accepting	4. To accept others					
	5. To respect others					
	9. To be open					
	6. To have trust					
	8. To be opened up to					
	11. To be close to others					
6. To be loved and understood	33. To be loved					
	3. To be respected					
	1. To be understood					
	2. To be accepted					
	7. To be liked					
7. To feel good and comfortable	30. To have stability					
	31. To feel comfortable					
	32. To feel happy					
	24. To feel good about self					
8. To achieve and help others	22. To achieve					
	25. To better myself					
	12. To help others					
	26. To be good					

Thought Unit (1-5 Scale) Ratings

Standard CCRT Categories
RESPONSES FROM OTHER
Date: ______
Rated by: ______
(Write in the thought unit →
Rate it and note P or N)

Edition 3 (clusters)	Edition 2					
1. Strong	24. Strong					
	23. Independent					
	29. Happy					
2. Controlling	26. Strict					
	20. Controlling					
3. Upset	16. Hurt					
	22. Dependent					
	28. Anxious					
	27. Angry					
	19. Out of control					
4. Bad	8. Not trustworthy					
	25. Bad					
5. Rejecting and opposing	7. Don't trust me					
	6. Don't respect me					
	2. Are not understanding					
	4. Rejecting					
	10. Dislike me					
	12. Distant					
	14. Unhelpful					
	17. Oppose me					
	15. Hurt me					

6. Helpful	13. Are helpful					
	18. Cooperative					
7. Likes me	30. Loves me					
	5. Respects me					
	9. Likes me					
	21. Gives me independence					
8. Understanding	11. Open					
	1. Understanding					
	3. Accepting					

Thought Unit (1–5 Scale) Ratings

Standard CCRT Categories
RESPONSES OF SELF
Date: ______
Rated by: ______
(Write in the thought unit →
Rate it and note P or N)

Edition 3 (clusters)	Edition 2					
1. Helpful	7. Am open					
	1. Understand					
	9. Am helpful					
2. Unreceptive	2. Don't understand					
	8. Am not open					
	6. Dislike others					
3. Respected and accepted	28. Feel comfortable					
	29. Feel happy					
	30. Feel loved					
	4. Feel respected					
	3. Feel accepted					
	5. Like others					

4. Oppose and hurt others	11. Oppose others					
	10. Hurt others					
5. Self-controlled and self-confident	14. Self-controlled					
	15. Independent					
	18. Self-confident					
	12. Controlling					
6. Helpless	13. Out of control					
	17. Helpless					
	19. Uncertain					
	16. Dependent					
7. Disappointed and depressed	21. Angry					
	20. Disappointed					
	22. Depressed					
	23. Unloved					
	24. Jealous					
8. Anxious and ashamed	27. Anxious					
	26. Ashamed					
	25. Guilty					

Adapted from Luborsky, L. (1998). A guide to the CCRT method. In L. Luborsky and P. Crits-Christoph (Eds.), *Understanding transference: The Core Conflictual Relationship Theme method* (2nd ed., pp. 15–42). Washington, DC: American Psychological Association.

Appendix B

Helping Alliance Questionnaire–I

THE HELPING ALLIANCE RELATIONSHIP QUESTIONNAIRE–I (HAQ-I): SELF-RATINGS OF THE HELPING ALLIANCE

Please judge each statement about your present relationship with your therapist. Mark each statement according to how strongly you feel that it is true, or not true, in this relationship. Please mark every one, with +3, +2, +1 or –1, –2, –3, to stand for the following answer:

EXAMPLES:

Positive	Negative
+3. Yes, I strongly feel that it is true.	–1. No, I feel that it is probably untrue, or more untrue than true.
+2. Yes, I feel it is true.	–2. No, I feel it is not true.
+1. Yes, I feel that it is probably true, or more true than untrue.	–3. No, I strongly feel that it is not true.

1. I believe that my therapist is helping me.
2. I believe that the treatment is helping me.
3. I have obtained some new understanding.
4. I have been feeling better recently.
5. I can already see that I will eventually work out the problems I came to treatment for.
6. I feel I can depend upon my therapist.
7. I feel the therapist understands me.
8. I feel the therapist wants me to achieve my goals.
9. I feel I am working together with the therapist in a joint effort.

10. I believe we have similar ideas about the nature of my problems.
11. I feel now that I can understand myself and deal with myself on my own (i.e., even if the therapist and I were no longer meeting for treatment appointments).

Kind of Change:

I feel improved in the following ways:______________________________

____

I feel worse in the following ways:_________________________________

____

Estimate of improvement so far:

1	2	3	4	5
None	Some	Moderate	Much	Very Much

NOTE: The Helping Alliance Questionnaire–II (HAq-II) can be found in chapter 7 (table 7.3).

Appendix C

Rating Scales for SE and SE Session-Limited Psychotherapy

THE MAIN SE TECHNIQUES (IN THE BEGINNING, MIDDLE, AND TOWARD THE END)

These rating scales are aimed at backing one purpose of the manual: to further specify SE psychotherapy. This psychotherapy is patient centered in the sense that the therapist listens, understands, responds, and listens again mainly on the basis of what the patient is saying, rather than on the basis of responses prepared in advance and based on theoretical allegiances. In this psychotherapy, the therapist and patient take a problem-solving approach to the meaning of the symptoms and the related interpersonal problems.

Supportive Techniques

The therapist must decide both initially and as the treatment progresses whether the treatment can rely primarily on expressive techniques or whether additional attention to the giving of support is needed. For some patients, the therapist gives enough support to maximize the patient's expressiveness. The most central ways of providing support and strengthening the alliance include conveying a sense of sympathetic understanding and helping the patient maintain vital defenses and activities that bolster areas of competence; each demonstrates a realistically hopeful attitude and recognizes the patient's ability to use the treatment tools and do what the therapist does as the therapist engages with the patient in a joint search for understanding.

General Scales

There are four scales for the degree to which a psychotherapy fits the characteristics of SE psychotherapy: three for the main distinctive qualities of SE and a fourth for an overall rating. These four scales were successfully used to try to distinguish samples of supportive-expressive psychotherapy, cognitive-behavioral psychotherapy, and drug counseling (Luborsky, Woody, McLellan, O'Brien, & Rosenzweig, 1982; Woody et al., 1983).

1. *The degree to which the treatment is focused on the therapist who is providing support:* by developing a helping alliance, through bolstering areas of competence, and by encouraging and supporting healthy defenses and activities

1	2	3	4	5
None	Some	Moderate	Much	Very Much

2. *The degree to which the treatment is focused on facilitating expressiveness:* as part of the search for understanding

1	2	3	4	5
None	Some	Moderate	Much	Very Much

3. *The degree to which the treatment is focused on the understanding of the relationship with the therapist:* and its basis in the transference pattern

1	2	3	4	5
None	Some	Moderate	Much	Very Much

4. *The degree to which the treatment fits the manual's specifications of supportive-expressive psychotherapy* ("adherence")

1	2	3	4	5
None	Some	Moderate	Much	Very Much

SPECIFIC SCALES

Rating Scales for Supportiveness: The Therapist's Way of Facilitating the Helping Alliance, Type 1

1. Conveying through words and manner support for the patient's wish to achieve the patient's goals

1	2	3	4	5
None	Some	Moderate	Much	Very Much

2. Conveying a sense of understanding and acceptance

1	2	3	4	5
None	Some	Moderate	Much	Very Much

3. Developing a liking for the patient

1	2	3	4	5
None	Some	Moderate	Much	Very Much

4. Assisting the patient to maintain vital defenses and to maintain activities that bolster morale, areas of competence, and general level of functioning

1	2	3	4	5
None	Some	Moderate	Much	Very Much

Expressive Techniques

The therapist follows the flow of the patient's thoughts in order to discern the meaning of the symptoms and the associated relationship problems as expressed in the Core Conflictual Relationship Theme (CCRT). During each session, the therapist is successively (1) listening, (2) understanding in terms of the formulation, (3) responding to what the patient is saying, and then (4) listening again.

1. Engaging in a joint search for understanding: HA, type 2

1	2	3	4	5
None	Some	Moderate	Much	Very Much

2. Understanding the patient's main symptoms, main sources of psychic pain, and changes in these

1	2	3	4	5
None	Some	Moderate	Much	Very Much

3. Attending by interpretations to each of the three spheres of the relationship triad: (1) current relationships in treatment, (2) current relationships out of treatment, and (3) past relationships

1	2	3	4	5
None	Some	Moderate	Much	Very Much

4. Seeing the symptoms as a solution and attempts at coping with a problem

1	2	3	4	5
None	Some	Moderate	Much	Very Much

5. Attending to the patient's perception of the therapist's behavior

1	2	3	4	5
None	Some	Moderate	Much	Very Much

RATING SCALES FOR EXPRESSIVE AIMS: THE THERAPIST'S ADEQUACY OF RESPONDING

1. The degree to which the therapist's response deals effectively with *a facet* of the main relationship problem—the Core Conflictual Relationship Theme (CCRT) problem

1	2	3	4	5
None	Some	Moderate	Much	Very Much

2. The degree to which the therapist also relates the CCRT to one of the symptoms

1	2	3	4	5
None	Some	Moderate	Much	Very Much

3. The degree to which the therapist's responses are directed to the most emotion-laden or pressing part of the patient's transference issue

1	2	3	4	5
None	Some	Moderate	Much	Very Much

4. The degree to which the therapist's responses recurrently recognize and deal adequately with a facet of the CCRT so as to facilitate the working through

1	2	3	4	5
None	Some	Moderate	Much	Very Much

5. The degree to which the therapist recognizes the patient's need to test the relationship in transference terms

1	2	3	4	5
None	Some	Moderate	Much	Very Much

6. The degree to which the therapist's responses pass the matching-of-messages test—they match the message of the patient with that of the therapist

1	2	3	4	5
None	Some	Moderate	Much	Very Much

a. State in a sentence the essence of the patient's main message in the session in CCRT terms:

b. State in a sentence the essence of the therapist's responses in the session in CCRT terms:

7. The degree to which the therapist's message is an adequate and effective response to the patient's message

1	2	3	4	5
None (misses the main point)	Some	Moderate	Much	Very Much (hits on the main point)

8. The degree to which the therapist's response is directed to the part of the transference issue that is closest to the patient's awareness

1	2	3	4	5
None	Some	Moderate	Much	Very Much

9. The degree to which the therapist presents responses in a form that is appropriately simple and noncomplex so as to be maximally understandable to the patient

1	2	3	4	5
None (unclear, overcomplex)	Some	Moderate	Much	Very Much (clear and simple)

10. The degree to which the therapist's responses are free of countertransference distortions

1	2	3	4	5
None (not free of distortion)	Some	Moderate (free of them)	Much	Very Much (free of distortion)

RATING SCALES FOR THE THERAPIST'S SKILL

1. The degree to which the therapist is conducting this treatment skillfully and competently

1	2	3	4	5
None	Some	Moderate	Much	Very Much

2. Rating scale for degree of help provided to the patient: the degree to which the patient believes the therapist is providing help. For example: "I was

pleased with the new understanding you gave me in the last session" or "I am really happy with the help I'm getting from you."

1	2	3	4	5
None or None	Some	Moderate	Much	Very Much

References

Aine, C. J. (1995). A conceptual overview and critique of functional neuroimaging techniques in humans: 1. MRI/fMRI and PET. *Critical Reviews of Neurobiology, 9,* 229–309.

Ainsworth, M. S., Blehar, M. C., Waters, E., & Wall, S. (1978). *Patterns of attachment: A psychological study of the strange situation.* Oxford, England: Lawrence Erlbaum.

Albani, C., Pokorny, D., Blaser, G., Gruninger, S., Konig, S., Marschke, F., Geissler, I., Koerner, A., Guyer, M., & Kaechele, H. (2002). A reformulation of the core conflictual relationship theme (CCRT categories): The CCRT-LU category system. *Psychotherapy Research, 12,* 319–338.

Alexander, F., & French, T. (1946). *Psychoanalytic therapy: Principles and applications.* New York: Ronald Press.

Alexander, L., & Luborsky, L. (1986). Research on the helping alliance. In L. Greenberg & W. Pinsof (Eds.), *The psychotherapeutic process: A research handbook* (pp. 325–366). New York: Guilford.

American Psychiatric Association. (1994). *Diagnostic and statistical manual of mental disorders* (4th ed.). Washington, DC.

Armelius, B., Gerin, P., & Luborsky, L. (1985). Clinician's judgment of mental health: An international validation of HSRS. *Department of Applied Psychology Reports, 13,* 1–10.

Auerbach, A. H., & Luborsky, L. (1968). Accuracy of judgments of psychotherapy and the nature of the "good hour." In J. Shlien, H. F. Hunt, J. P. Matarazzo, and C. Savage (Eds.), *Research in psychotherapy, Vol. 3* (pp. 155–168). Washington, DC: American Psychological Association.

Balint, M., Ornstein, P., & Balint, E. (1977). *Focal psychotherapy.* London: Tavistock.

Barber, J. P., Connolly, M. B., Crits-Christoph, P., Gladis, L., & Siqueland, L. (2000). Alliance predicts patients' outcome beyond in-treatment change in symptoms. *Journal of Consulting and Clinical Psychology, 68,* 1027–1032.

Barber, J. P., & Crits-Christoph, P. (1996). Development of an adherence/competence scale for dynamic therapy: Preliminary findings. *Psychotherapy Research, 6,* 81–94.

Barber, J. P., Krakauer, I., Calvo, N., Badgio, P. C., & Faude, J. (1997). Measuring adherence and competence of dynamic therapists in the treatment of cocaine dependence. *Journal of Psychotherapy Practice and Research, 6,* 12–24.

Barber, J. P., Luborsky, L., Crits-Christoph, P., & Diguer, L. (1995). A comparison of core conflictual relationship themes before psychotherapy and during early sessions. *Journal of Counseling and Clinical Psychology, 63,* 145–148.

Barber, J. P., Moras, K., Krakauer, I., Calvo, N., Badgio, P. C., & Faude, J. (1997). Measuring adherence and competence of dynamic therapists in the treatment of cocaine dependence. *Journal of Psychotherapy Practice and Research, 6,* 12–14.

Barrett-Lennard, G. T. (1962). Dimensions of the client's experience of his therapist associated with personality change. *Genetic Psychology Monographs, 76* (Monograph 43).

Beck, A. T., Rush, A., Shaw, B., & Emery, G. (1979). *Cognitive therapy of depression: A treatment manual.* (Copyright by A. T. Beck, 1978). Typescript.

Beck, A. T., Wright, F. D., Newman, C. F., & Liese, B. S. (1993). *Cognitive therapy of substance abuse.* New York: Guilford.

Benjamin, L. S. (1994). SASB: A bridge between personality theory and clinical psychology. *Psychological Inquiry, 5,* 273–316.

Bergin, A. E., & Lambert, M. J. (1978). The evaluation of therapeutic outcomes. In S. L. Garfield & A. E. Bergin (Eds.), *Handbook of psychotherapy and behavior change: An empirical analysis.* (2nd ed., pp. 139–189.) New York: Wiley.

Bergmann, M., & Hartman, F. (Eds.). (1977). *The evolution of psychoanalytic technique.* New York: Basic.

Berman, J. S., & Luborsky, L. (in preparation). Researcher allegiance, treatment credibility, and the outcome of comparisons between psychotherapies.

Bibring, E. (1954). Psychoanalysis and the dynamic psychotherapies. *Journal of the American Psychoanalytic Association, 2,* 745–770.

Binder, J., & Strupp, H. (1991). The Vanderbilt approach to time-limited dynamic psychotherapy. In P. Crits-Christoph & J. Barber (Eds.), *Handbook of short-term dynamic psychotherapy* (pp. 137–165). New York: Basic.

Blatt, S. (1999). Personality factors in brief treatment of depression: Further analyses of the NIMH-sponsored treatment for depression collaborative research project. In D. Janowsky (Ed.), *Psychotherapy: Indications and outcomes* (pp. 23–46). Washington, DC: American Psychiatric Press.

Blatt, S., & Felsen, I. (1993). Different kinds of folks may need different kinds of strokes: The effect of patients' characteristics on therapeutic process and outcome. *Psychotherapy Research, 3,* 245–259.

Blatt, S. J., & Zuroff, D. C. (1992). Interpersonal relatedness and self-definition: Two prototypes for depression. *Clinical Psychology Review, 12,* 527–562.

Blatt, S. J., Zuroff, D. C., Bondi, C. M., Sanislow, C. A., & Pilkonis, P. A. (1998). When and how perfectionism impedes the brief treatment of depression: Further analyses of the National Institute of Mental Health Treatment of Depression Collaborative Research Program. *Journal of Consulting and Clinical Psychology, 68,* 423–428.

Blomberg, J., Lazar, A., & Sandell, R. (2001). Long-term outcome of long-term psychoanalytically oriented therapies: First findings of the Stockholm outcome of psychotherapy and psychoanalysis study. *Psychotherapy Research, 11,* 361–382.

Bond, M., Banon, E., & Grenier, M. (1998). Differential effects of interventions on the therapeutic alliance with patients with personality disorders. *Journal of Psychotherapy Practice and Research, 7,* 301–318.

Book, H. (1998). *How to practice brief psychodynamic psychotherapy: The CCRT method.* Washington, DC: American Psychological Association.

Bowlby, J. (1982). *Attachment and loss, Vol. 1: Attachment.* New York: Basic Books.

——. (1988). *A secure base: Clinical application of attachment theory.* London: Routledge.

Brady, J. P. (1970). Behavior therapy. In J. H. Price (Ed.), *Modern trends in psychological medicine* (pp. 256–276). London: Butterworth.

Brenman, M. (1952). On teasing and being teased and the problem of "moral masochism." *Psychoanalytic Study of the Child, 7,* 264–285.

Brennan, K. A., Clark, C. L., & Shaver, P. R. (1998). Self-report measurement of adult attachment: An integrative overview. In J. A. Simpson & W. S. Rholes (Eds.), *Attachment theory and close relationships* (pp. 46–76). New York: Guilford.

Bucci, W. (1985). Dual coding: A cognitive model for psychoanalytic research. *Journal of the American Psychoanalytic Association, 33,* 571–607.

Buckley, P., Conte, H. R., Plutchik, R., Wild, K. V., & Karasu, T. B. (1984). Psychodynamic variables as predictors of psychotherapy outcome. *American Journal of Psychiatry, 141,* 742–748.

Butcher, J. N., & Koss, M. P. (1978). Research on brief and crisis-oriented therapies. In S. Garfield & A. Bergin (Eds.), *Handbook of psychotherapy and behavior change: An empirical analysis* (2nd ed., pp. 725–768). New York: Wiley.

Butler, J. M., & Rice, L. N. (1963). Audience, self-actualization and drive theory. In J. M. Wepman & R. W. Heine (Eds.), *Concepts of personality.* (pp. 79–110) Chicago: Aldine.

Butler, S. F., Flasher, L. V., & Strupp, H. H. (1993). Countertransference and qualities of the psychotherapist. In N. E. Miller & L. Luborsky (Eds.), *Psychodynamic treatment research: A handbook for clinical practice* (pp. 342–360). New York: Basic.

Carels, R. A., Cacciapaglia, H., Pérez-Benítez, C. I., Douglass, O., Christie, S., & O'Brien, W. H. (2003). The association between emotional upset and cardiac arrhythmia during daily life. *Journal of Consulting and Clinical Psychology, 71,* 613–618.

Cattell, R., & Luborsky, L. (1950). P-technique demonstrated as a new clinical method for determining personality and symptom structure. *Journal of General Psychology, 42,* 3–24.

Cohen, J. (1977). *Statistical power analysis for the behavioral sciences* (2nd ed.). New York: Academic Press.

Colby, K. M. (1951). *A primer for psychotherapists.* New York: Ronald Press.

Connolly, M. B., Crits-Christoph, P., Shappell, S., Barber, J. P., Luborsky, L., & Shaffer, C. (1999). Relation of transference interpretations to outcome in the early sessions of brief supportive-expressive psychotherapy. *Psychotherapy Research, 9,* 485–495.

Connolly Gibbons, M. B., Crits-Christoph, P., de la Cruz, C., Barber, J. P., Siqueland, L., & Gladis, M. (2003). Pretreatment expectations, interpersonal functioning, and symptoms in the prediction of the therapeutic alliance across supportive-expressive psychotherapy and cognitive therapy. *Psychotherapy Research, 13*, 59–76.

Constantino, M. J., Castonguay, L. G., & Schut, A. J. (2002). The working alliance: A flagship for the "scientist-practitioner" model in psychotherapy. In G. S. Tryon (Ed.), *Counseling based on process research: Applying what we know*. (pp. 81–131) Boston: Allyn and Bacon.

Crits-Christoph, P., Barnackie, K., Kurcias, J., Beck, A. T., Carroll, K., Perry, K., Luborsky, L., McLellan, A. T., Woody, G., Thompson, L., Gallagher, D., & Zitrin, C. (1991). Meta-analysis of therapist effects in psychotherapy outcome studies. *Psychotherapy Research, 1*, 81–91.

Crits-Christoph, P., Cooper, A., & Luborsky, L. (1988). The accuracy of therapists' interpretations and the outcome of dynamic psychotherapy. *Journal of Consulting and Clinical Psychology, 56*, 490–495.

——. (1990). The measurement of accuracy of interpretations. In L. Luborsky & P. Crits-Christoph (Eds.), *Understanding transference: The CCRT method* (pp. 173–188). New York: Basic.

——. (1998). The measurement of accuracy of interpretations. In L. Luborsky & P. Crits-Christoph (Eds.), *Understanding transference: The core conflictual relationship theme method* (pp. 197–212). Washington, DC: American Psychological Association.

Crits-Christoph, P., & Demorest, A. (1988). List of standard categories (Edition 2). Unpublished manuscript, University of Pennsylvania School of Medicine, Philadelphia.

Crits-Christoph, P., & Luborsky, L. (1988). Application of the CCRT: A measure of adequacy of therapist's interpretation and a measure of patient's self-understanding. In H. Dahl, H. Kaechele, & H. Thomae (Eds.), *Psychoanalytic process research strategies* (pp. 117– 128). New York: Springer.

Crits-Christoph, P., Siqueland, L., Chittams, J., Barber, J., Beck, A. T., Frank, A., Liese, B., Luborsky, L., Mark, D., Mercer, D., Onkon, L. S., Najavits, L. M., Thase, M. E., & Woody, G. (1998). Training in cognitive, supportive-expressive, and drug counseling therapies for cocaine dependence. *Journal of Consulting and Clinical Psychology, 66*, 484–492.

DeJonghe, F., Kool, S., Crits-Christoph, P., Crits-Christoph, K., Wolf-Palmero, D., Fichter, M., & Rudick, D. (1998). Brief supportive-expressive psychodynamic psychotherapy for generalized anxiety disorder. In J. P. Barber & P. Crits-Christoph (Eds.), *Dynamic therapies for psychiatric disorders* (Axis I, 43–83). New York: Basic.

DeJonghe, F., Kool, S., Van Aalst, G., Dekker, J., & Peen, J. (2001). Combining psychotherapy and antidepressants in the treatment of depression. *Journal of Affective Disorders, 64*, 217–229.

Derogatis, L. R., Lipman, R. S., Covi, I., Rickels, K., & Ublenhuth, E. H. (1970). Dimensions of outpatient neurotic pathology: Comparisons of a clinical versus an empirical assessment. *Journal of Consulting and Clinical Psychology, 34*, 164–171.

DeRubeis, R., Hollon, S., Evans, M., & Bemis, K. (1982). Can psychotherapies for depression be discriminated? A systematic investigation of cognitive therapy and interpersonal therapy. *Journal of Consulting and Clinical Psychology, 50,* 744–756.

Diguer, L., Barber, J. P., & Luborsky, L. (1993). Three concomitants: Personality disorder, psychiatric severity and outcome of dynamic psychotherapy of major depression. *American Journal of Psychiatry, 150,* 1246–1248.

DiMascio, A., Klerman, G., Weissman, M., Prusoff, B., Neu, C., & Moore, P. (1978). An ethically justifiable and methodological appropriate control group for psychotherapy research in acute depression. Typescript.

Docherty, J., Marder, S., Van Kammen, D., & Siris, S. (1977). Psychotherapy and pharmacotherapy: Conceptual issues. *American Journal of Psychiatry, 134,* 529–533.

Doss, B. D. (2004). Changing the way we study change in psychotherapy. *Clinical Psychology: Science and Practice, 11,* 368–386.

Elkin, I., Shea, T., Watkins, J., Imber, S., Sotsky, S., Colins, J., Glass, D., Pilkonis, P., Leber, W., Docherty, J., Fiester, S., & Parloff, M. (1989). National Institute of Mental Health Treatment of Depression Collaborative Research Program: General effectiveness of treatments. *Archives of General Psychiatry, 46,* 971–982.

Endicott, J., Nee, J., Harrison, W., & Blumenthal, R. (1993). Quality of Life, Enjoyment, and Satisfaction Scale: A new measure. *Psychopharmacology Bulletin, 29,* 321–326.

Endicott, J., Spitzer, R., Fleiss, J., & Cohen, J. (1976). The Global Assessment Scale: A procedure for measuring overall severity of psychiatric disturbance. *Archives of General Psychiatry, 33,* 766–771.

Fenichel, O. (1938). Problems of psychoanalytic technique. *The Psychoanalytic Quarterly,* 7 421–442.

Fenichel, O. (1939). Problems of psychoanalytic technique. *The Psychoanalytic Quarterly, 8,* 57–87; 164–185; 303–324; 438–470.

Ferenczi, S. (1950). *Further contribution to the theory and technique of psychoanalysis.* London: Hogarth.

Fonagy, P. (1991). An open-door revision of outcome studies in psychoanalysis. Report presented by the research committee of the IPA, at the request of the president. Retrieved May 20, 2003, from http://www.ipa.org.uk.

Fonagy, P. (2001). *Attachment theory and psychoanalysis*. New York: Other Press.

Fonagy, P. (2003). Attachment theory and psychoanalysis. *Journal of Child Psychotherapy, 29*(1), 109–120.

Francis, M., Luborsky, L., Rosenthal, R., Diguer, L., Kirk, D., German, R., Cacciola, J., Popp, C., & Faude, J. (in preparation). Narratives told *spontaneously* during psychotherapy sessions (RE method) versus narratives *requested* during an interview (RAP method).

Frank, J. (1968). The role of hope in psychotherapy. *International Journal of Psychiatry, 5,* 383–395.

French, T., & Wheeler, D. (1963). Hope and the repudiation of hope in psychoanalytic therapy. *International Journal of Psychoanalysis, 44,* 304–316.

Freud, S. (1900/1953). The interpretation of dreams. In J. Strachey (Ed. & Trans.), *The standard edition of the complete psychological works of Sigmund Freud* (Vols. 4 & 5). London: Hogarth.

——. (1911/1958). The handling of dream-interpretation in psychoanalysis. In J. Strachey (Ed. and Trans.), *The standard edition of the complete psychological works of Sigmund Freud* (Vol. 12, pp. 89–96). London: Hogarth.

——. (1912a/1958). The dynamics of transference. In J. Strachey (Ed. and Trans.), *The standard edition of the complete psychological works of Sigmund Freud* (Vol. 12, pp. 97–108). London: Hogarth.

——. (1912b/1958). Recommendations to physicians practicing psychoanalysis. In J. Strachey (Ed. and Trans.), *The standard edition of the complete psychological works of Sigmund Freud* (Vol. 12, pp. 109–120). London: Hogarth.

——. (1913a/1958). On beginning the treatment (further recommendations on the technique of psychoanalysis). In J. Strachey (Ed. and Trans.), *The standard edition of the complete psychological works of Sigmund Freud* (Vol. 12, pp. 121–144). London: Hogarth.

——. (1913b/1958). The claims of psychoanalysis to the interest of the non-psychological sciences. In J. Strachey (Ed. & Trans.), *The standard edition of the complete psychological works of Sigmund Freud* (Vol. 13, pp. 165–192). London: Hogarth.

——. (1914/1958). Remembering, repeating and working through. In J. Strachey (Ed. & Trans.), *The standard edition of the complete psychological works of Sigmund Freud* (Vol. 12, pp. 145–156). London: Hogarth.

——. (1915a/1957). The unconscious. In J. Strachey (Ed. & Trans.), *The standard edition of the complete psychological works of Sigmund Freud* (Vol. 16, pp. 166–204). London: Hogarth.

——. (1915b/1958). Observations on transference-love: Further recommendations on the technique of psychoanalysis. In J. Strachey (Ed. & Trans.), *The standard edition of the complete psychological works of Sigmund Freud* (Vol. 16, pp. 431–447). London: Hogarth.

——. (1917/1957). Mourning and melancholia. In J. Strachey (Ed. & Trans.), *The standard edition of the complete psychological works of Sigmund Freud* (Vol. 14, pp. 243–258). London: Hogarth.

——. (1917/1963). Transference. In J. Strachey (Ed. & Trans.), *The standard edition of the complete psychological works of Sigmund Freud* (Vol. 16, pp. 431–447). London: Hogarth.

——. (1926/1959). Inhibitions, symptoms, and anxiety. In J. Strachey (Ed. & Trans.), *The standard edition of the complete psychological works of Sigmund Freud* (Vol. 20, pp. 87–174). London: Hogarth.

——. (1932/1964). The dissection of the psychical personality. In J. Strachey (Ed. & Trans.), *The standard edition of the complete psychological works of Sigmund Freud* (Vol. 22, pp. 57–80). London: Hogarth.

——. (1937/1964). Analysis terminable and interminable. In J. Strachey (Ed. & Trans.), *The standard edition of the complete psychological works of Sigmund Freud* (Vol. 23, pp. 216–254). London: Hogarth.

Fried, D., Crits-Christoph, P., & Luborsky, L. (1992). The first empirical demonstration of transference in psychotherapy. *Journal of Nervous and Mental Disease, 180,* 326–331.

Frisch, M. B., Cornell, J., Billanueea, M., & Retzlaff, P. J. (1992). Clinical validation of the Quality of Life Inventory: A measure of life's satisfaction for use in treatment planning and outcome assessment. *Psychological Assessment, 4,* 92–101.

Gabbard, G. (2001). *Treatments of psychiatric disorders* (3rd ed.). Washington, DC: American Psychiatric Press.

Gaston, L. (1991). Reliability and criterion-related validity of the California Psychotherapy Alliance Scales—Patient version. *Psychological Assessment, 3,* 68–74.

Gaston, L., Thompson, L., Gallagher, D., Cournoyer, L. G., & Gagnon, R. (1998). Alliance, technique, and their interactions in predicting outcome of behavioral, cognitive, and brief dynamic therapy. *Psychotherapy Research, 8,* 190–209.

George, C., Kaplan, N., & Main, M. (1985). *The attachment interview for adults.* Unpublished manuscript, University of California, Berkeley.

Gerin, P., Baguet, J., & Sali, H. (in preparation). Measuring change in psychotherapy by the core conflictual relationship theme method.

Gill, M. M. (1951). Ego psychology and psychotherapy. *Psychoanalytic Quarterly, 20,* 60–71.

———. (1954). Psychoanalysis and exploratory psychoanalysis. *Journal of the American Psychoanalytic Association, 2,* 771–790.

———. (1979). The analysis of the transference. *Journal of the American Psychoanalytic Association* (Supplement), *27,* 263–288.

———. (1982). Analysis of transference. *Theory and Technique. Psychological Issues,* Monograph 53. New York: International Universities Press.

Gill, M. M., & Hoffman, I. Z. (1982). A method for studying the analysis of aspects of the patient's experience of the relationship in psychoanalysis and psychotherapy. *Journal of the American Psychoanalytic Association, 30*(1), 137–167.

Glover, E. (1955). *The technique of psycho-analysis.* New York: International Universities Press.

Greenberg, L. (2002). Integrating an emotion-focused approach to treatment into psychotherapy integration. *Journal of Psychotherapy Integration, 12,* 154–189.

Greenblatt, M. (1959). Discussion of papers by Saslow and Matarazzo and Lacey. In E. Rubinstein & M. Parloff (Eds.), *Research in psychotherapy* (pp. 209–220). Washington, DC: American Psychological Association.

Greenson, R. (1965). The working alliance and transference neurosis. *Psychoanalytic Quarterly, 34,* 18–81.

———. (1967). *The technique and practice of psychoanalysis* (Vol. I). New York: International Universities Press.

Greenspan, S. (1981). Psychopathology and adaptation in infancy and early childhood: Principles of clinical diagnosis and preventive intervention. *Clinical Infant Reports,* No. 1. New York: International Universities Press.

Grenyer, B. F. S. (2002). *Mastering relationship conflicts: Discoveries in theory, research and practice.* Washington, DC: American Psychological Association.

Grinker, R., & Spiegel, J. (1944). Brief psychotherapy in war neuroses. *Psychosomatic Medicine, 6,* 123–131.

Grinker, R., & Spiegel, J. (1945). *Men under stress.* Philadelphia: Blakiston.

Group for the Advancement of Psychiatry. (1975). Pharmacotherapy and psychotherapy: Paradoxes, problems and progress. Report 93. New York: GAP.

Henry, W., Sims, J., & Spray, S. (1973). *Public and private lives of psychotherapists.* San Francisco: Jossey-Bass.

Herink, R. (Ed.). (1980). *The psychotherapy handbook: The A to Z guide to more than 250 different therapies in use today.* New York: New American Library (Meridian).

Hilsenroth, M., Ackerman, S. J., Blaggs, M. D., Balty, M. R., & Money, M. A. (2003). Short-term psychodynamic psychotherapy for depression: An examination of statistical, clinically-significant, and technique-specific change. *Journal of Nervous and Mental Disorders, 191,* 349–357.

Hollender, M. H. (1965). *The practice of psychoanalytic psychotherapy.* New York: Grune & Stratton.

Holt, R., & Luborsky, L. (1958). *Personality patterns of psychiatrists* (Vol. I). New York: Basic.

Holt, R. R. (Ed.) (1968) *Diagnostic psychological testing* (Rev. ed.) New York: International Universities Press.

Horowitz, M. (1979). *States of mind: Analysis of change in psychotherapy.* New York: Plenum.

Horowitz, M., Marmar, C., & Wilner, N. (1979). Analysis of patient states and state transitions. *Journal of Nervous and Mental Disease, 167,* 91–99.

Horvath, A., Gaston, L., & Luborsky, L. (1993). The therapeutic alliance and its measures. In N. Miller, L. Luborsky, J. P. Barber, & J. Docherty (Eds.), *Psychodynamic treatment research: A handbook for clinical practice* (pp. 247–273). New York: Basic.

Horvath, A. O. (1982). *Working alliance* (Rev. ed.). Unpublished manuscript, Simon Fraser University, Vancouver, British Columbia, Canada.

Horvath, A. O., & Symonds, B. D. (1991). Relation between working alliance and outcome in psychotherapy: A meta-analysis. *Journal of Counseling Psychology, 38,* 139–149.

Jacob, S., Bernhard, M., Delgado, A., & Strain, J. (1977). Screening for organic mental syndrome in the medically ill. *Annals of Internal Medicine, 86,* 40.

Janis, I. (Ed.). (1982). *Counseling on personal decisions: Theory and research on short-term helping relationships.* New Haven: Yale University Press.

——. (1983). *Short term counseling: Guidelines based on recent research.* New Haven: Yale University Press.

Karasu, T. B. (1981). From Freudian psychoanalysis to experiential psychotherapies: An essay on recent trends. *Academy Forum, 25,* 13–31.

Kay, J., & Gabbard, G. O. (2003). The fate of integrated treatment: Whatever happened to the biopsychosocial psychiatrist? Reply. *American Journal of Psychiatry, 160,* 186.

Kernberg, O. (1975). *Borderline conditions and pathological narcissism.* New York: Jason Aronson.

——. (1984). *Severe personality disorders: Psychotherapeutic strategies.* New Haven: Yale University Press.

Kernberg, O., Burstein, E., Coyne, L., Applebaum, A., Horowitz, L., & Voth, H. (1972). Psychotherapy and psychoanalysis: Final report of the Menninger Foundation's psychotherapy research project. *Bulletin of the Menninger Clinic, 36,* 1–275.

Kihlstrom, J. F., & Kihlstrom, L. C. (1998). Integrating science and practice in an environment of managed care. In D. K. Routh & R. J. DeRubeis (Eds.), *The science of clinical psychology: Accomplishments and future directions* (pp. 281–293). Washington, DC: American Psychological Association.

Klein, G. (1970). *Perception, motives and personality.* New York: Knopf.

Klerman, G., Rounsaville, B., Chevron, E., Neu, C., & Weissman, M. (1979). *Manual for short-term interpersonal psychotherapy (IPT) for depression.* New Haven: Yale University Press.

Klerman, G., Weissman, M., Rounsaville, B., & Chevron, E. (1984). *Interpersonal psychotherapy of depression.* New York: Guilford.

Klerman, G. L., Weissman, M. M., Markowitz, J. C., Glick, I., Wilma, P. J., Mason, B., & Shear, M. K. (1994). In A. E. Bergin & S. L. Garfield (Eds.), *Medications and psychotherapy* (pp. 734–782). New York: Wiley.

Knight, R. P. (1949). A critique of the present status of the psychotherapies. *Bulletin of the New York Academy of Medicine, 25,* 100–114.

Kohut, H. (1977). *The restoration of the self.* New York: International Universities Press.

Koss, M., & Shiang, J. (1994). Research on brief psychotherapy. In A. Bergin & S. Garfield (Eds.), *Handbook of psychotherapy and behavior change* (pp. 664–700). New York: Wiley.

Lambert, M., Shapiro, D. A., & Bergin, A. (1986). The effectiveness of psychotherapy. In S. Garfield & A. Bergin (Eds.), *Handbook of psychotherapy and behavior change* (pp. 157–212). New York: Wiley.

Lambert, M. J., & Bergin, A. E. (1994). The effectiveness of psychotherapy. In A. E. Bergin & S. L. Garfield (Eds.), *Handbook of psychotherapy and behavior change* (pp. 143–149). New York: Wiley.

Levine, F. J., & Luborsky, L. (1981). The core conflictual relationship theme: A demonstration of reliable clinical inference by the method of mismatched cases. In S. Tuttman, C. Kaye, & M. Zimmerman (Eds.), *Object and self: A developmental approach* (pp. 501–526). New York: International Universities Press.

Liebowitz, J. H., Rembar, J. C., Kernberg, P. F., Frankel, A. K., & Kruger, R. S. (1988). Judging mental health-sickness in children: Development of a rating scale. *Journal of the American Academy of Child and Adolescent Psychiatry, 27,* 193–199.

Lindemann, E. (1944). Symptomatology and management of acute grief. *American Journal of Psychiatry, 101,* 141–148.

Lipton, S. (1979). An addendum to: The advantages of Freud's techniques as shown in his analysis of the Rat Man. *International Journal of Psychoanalysis, 60,* 215–216.

Loughead, J., Luborsky, L., Gur, R., Weingarten, C. P., German, R., Kirk, D., & Krause, B. (in preparation). Brain activation during silent reading of one's own narratives: fMRI evidence from a core conflictual relationship theme approach.

Luborsky, E. B. (1999). *My teacher has your voice: The language of attachment.* Paper presented at the Spring meeting of the American Psychological Association, Division 39, New York.

Luborsky, E. B. (2001). "No talking!" The possibility in play. *Journal of Clinical Psychoanalysis, 10*(3/4), 445–459.

Luborsky, L. (1953). Intraindividual repetitive measurements (P-Technique) in understanding psychotherapeutic change. In O. H. Mowrer (Ed.), *Psychotherapy: Theory and research.* (pp. 389–413) New York: Ronald Press.

———. (1962). Clinician's judgements of mental health: A proposed scale. *Archives of General Psychiatry, 7,* 407–417.

———. (1964). A psychoanalytic research on momentary forgetting during free association. *Bulletin of the Philadelphia Association for Psychoanalysis, 14,* 119–137.

———. (1967). Momentary forgetting during psychotherapy and psychoanalysis: A theory and research method. In R. R. Holt (Ed.), *Motives and thought: Psychoanalytic essays in honor of David Rapaport* (pp. 177–217). New York: International Universities Press.

———. (1969). Research cannot yet influence clinical practice. (An evaluation of Strupp and Bergin's *Some empirical and conceptual bases for coordinated research in psychotherapy: Critical review of issues, trends and evidence.*) *International Journal of Psychiatry, 7,* 135–140.

———. (1973). The task of the psychotherapist: A Socratic dialogue between the therapist and the supervisor in psychoanalytically oriented psychotherapy. Typescript.

———. (1976). Helping alliances in psychotherapy: The groundwork for a study of their relationship to its outcome. In J. L. Claghorn (Ed.), *Successful psychotherapy* (pp. 92–116). New York: Brunner/Mazel.

———. (1977). Measuring a pervasive psychic structure in psychotherapy: The core conflictual relationship theme. In N. Freedman & S. Grand (Eds.), *Communicative structures and psychic structures* (pp. 367–395). New York: Plenum.

———. (1978). The relationship anecdotes paradigms test (RAP test): A TAT-like method using actual narratives. Typescript.

———. (1979). *Manual for nonscheduled minimal treatment* (Adapted from A. DiMascio, G. Klerman, M. Weissman, B. Prusoff, C. Neu, & P. Moore. [1978].). Typescript.

———. (1984). *Principles of psychoanalytic psychotherapy: A manual for supportive-expressive (SE) treatment.* New York: Basic.

———. (1990). Theory and technique in dynamic psychotherapy: Curative factors and training therapists to maximize them. *Psychotherapy and psychosomatics, 53,* 50–57.

———. (1992). Does psychotherapy research really offer good ideas for psychotherapists? *Journal of Psychotherapy: Practice and Research, 1,* 310–312.

———. (1994). Therapeutic alliances as predictors of psychotherapy outcomes: Factors explaining the predictive success. In A. Horvath & L. Greenberg (Eds.), *The working alliance: Therapy, research and practice* (pp. 38–50). New York: Wiley.

———. (1995). The first trial of P technique in psychotherapy research: A still-lively legacy. *Journal of Consulting and Clinical Psychology, 63,* 6–14.

———. (1996). *The symptom-context method: Symptoms as opportunities in psychotherapy.* Washington, DC: American Psychological Association.

———. (1997). The core conflictual relationship theme (CCRT): A basic case formulation method. In T. Eells (Ed.), *Handbook of psychotherapy case formulation* (pp. 58–83). New York: Guilford.

———. (1998). A guide to the CCRT method. In L. Luborsky & P. Crits-Christoph (Eds.), *Understanding transference: The core conflictual relationship theme method* (2nd ed., pp. 15–42). Washington, DC: American Psychological Association.

———. (1998). The relationship anecdotes paradigm (RAP) interview as a versatile source of narratives. In L. Luborsky & P. Crits-Christoph (Eds.), *Understanding transference: The core conflictual relationship theme method* (2nd ed., pp. 109–120). Washington, DC: American Psychological Association.

———. (2000a). A pattern-setting therapeutic alliance study revisited ("Helping alliances in psychotherapy"). In J. Claghorn (Ed.), *Successful psychotherapy* (pp. 92–111). New York: Brunner/Mazel.

———. (2000b). Psychoanalytic psychotherapies. In A. F. Kazdin (Ed.), *Encyclopedia of Psychotherapy*. Washington, DC: Oxford University Press.

———. (2001). The meaning of empirically supported treatment research for psychoanalytic and other long term therapies. *Psychoanalytic Dialogues, 11*, 583–604.

———. (2002). Supportive-expressive dynamic psychotherapy: Its central principles, procedures, and empirical supports. *Encyclopedia of Psychotherapy, 2*, 1–6.

Luborsky, L., & Auerbach, A. H. (1969). The symptom-context method: Quantitative studies of symptom formation in psychotherapy. *Journal of the American Psychoanalytic Association, 17*, 68–99.

Luborsky, L., & Bachrach, H. (1974). Factors influencing clinician's judgments of mental health: Eighteen experiences with the Health-Sickness Rating Scale. *Archives of General Psychiatry, 31*, 292–299.

Luborsky, L., Bachrach, H., Graff, H., Pulver, S., & Christoph, P. (1979). Preconditions and consequences of transference interpretations: A clinical-quantitative investigation. *Journal of Nervous and Mental Disease, 167*, 391–401.

Luborsky, L., Barber, J. P., Siqueland, L., Johnson, S., Najavits, L. M., Frank, A., Daley, D. (1996). The revised Helping Alliance Questionnaire–II (HAq-II): Psychometric properties. *Journal of Psychotherapy Research and Practice, 6*, 260–271.

Luborsky, L., & Barrett, M. S. (2006). Theoretical allegiance. In J. C. Norcross, L. E. Beutler, & R. F. Levant (Eds.), *Evidence-based practices in mental health: Debate and dialogue on the fundamental questions*. (pp. 257–267) Washington, DC: American Psychological Association.

Luborsky, L., Barrett, M. S., Rosenthal, R., Diguer, L., Berman, J. S., Andrusyna, T., Shapiro, D. A., & Crooks, M. L. (in preparation). The history and empirical status of key psychoanalytic concepts.

Luborsky, L., & Crits-Christoph, P. (1990). *Understanding transference: The core conflictual relationship theme method.* New York: Basic.

———. (1998). *Understanding transference: The core conflictual relationship theme method* (2nd ed.). Washington, DC: American Psychological Association.

Luborsky, L., Crits-Christoph, P., Alexander, L., Margolis, M., & Cohen, M. (1983). Two helping alliance methods for predicting outcomes of psychotherapy: A counting signs vs. a global rating method. *Journal of Nervous and Mental Disorders, 171*, 480–492.

Luborsky, L., Crits-Christoph, P., McLellan, T., Woody, G., Piper, W., Imber, S., & Liberman, B. (1986). Do therapists vary much in their success? Findings from four outcome studies. *American Journal of Orthopsychiatry, 56*, 501–512.

Luborsky, L., Crits-Christoph, P., Mintz, J., & Auerbach, A. (1988). *Who will benefit from psychotherapy? Predicting therapeutic outcomes.* New York: Basic.

Luborsky, L., & DeRubeis, R. (1984). The use of psychotherapy manuals: A small revolution in psychotherapy research style. *Clinical Psychology Review, 4*, 5–14.

Luborsky, L., & Diguer, L. (1995). A novel CCRT reliability study: Reply to Zander et al. *Psychotherapy Research, 5*, 237–241.

Luborsky, L., Diguer, L., Andrusyna, T., Friedman, S., Tarca, C., Popp, C. A., Ermold, J., & Silberschatz, G. (2004). A method of choosing CCRT scorers. *Psychotherapy Research, 14*, 127–134.

Luborsky, L., Diguer, L., Kaechele, H., Dahlbender, R., Waldinger, R., Freni, S., Krause, R., Frevert, G., Bucci, W., Drouin, M. S., Fischman, N. T., Seganti, A., Wischmann, T., Hori, S., Azzonne, P., Pokorny, D., Staats, H., Zobel, H., Grenyer, B., Soldz, S., Anstadt, T., Schauenburg, H., Benninghoven, D., Stigler, M., & Tschesnova, I. (1999). A guide to the CCRT's methods, discoveries and future. Retrieved from http://sip.medizin.uni-ulm.de/Psychotherapie/ccrtframe.html.

Luborsky, L., Diguer, L., Luborsky, E., McLellan, A. T., Woody, G., & Alexander, L. (1993). Psychological health-sickness as a predictor of the outcomes of psychotherapy. *Journal of Consulting and Clinical Psychology, 61*, 542–548.

Luborsky, L., Diguer, L., McLellan, T. A., Woody, G., & Seligman, D. A. (1997). The psychotherapist matters: Comparison of outcomes across 22 therapists and 7 patient samples. *Clinical Psychology: Science and Practice, 4*, 53–65.

Luborsky, L., Diguer, L., Seligman, D. A., Rosenthal, R., Krause, E. D., Johnson, S., Halperin, G., Bishop, M., Berman, J. S., & Schweizer, E. (1999). The researcher's own therapy allegiances: A "wild card" in comparisons of treatment efficacy. *Clinical Psychology: Science and Practice, 6*, 95–132.

Luborsky, L., Docherty, J. P., Barber, J. P., & Miller, N. (1993). How this basic handbook helps the partnership of clinicians and clinical researchers: Preface. In N. Miller, L. Luborsky, J. P. Barber, & J. P. Docherty (Eds.), *Psychodynamic treatment research: A handbook for clinical practice* (pp. xix-xxvi). New York: Basic.

Luborsky, L., Fabian, M., Hall, B. H., Ticho, E., & Ticho, G. R. (1958). Treatment variables. *Bulletin of the Menninger Clinic, 22*, 126–147.

Luborsky, L., Luborsky, E., Diguer, L., Schmidt, K., Dengler, D., Schaffler, P., Faude, J., Morris, M., Buchsbaum, H., Emde, R. (1996). Extending the core relationship theme into early childhood. In G. G. Noam & K. W. Fischer (Eds.), *Development and vulnerability in close relationships* (pp. 287–308). The Jean Piaget symposium series. Hillsdale, NJ: Lawrence Erlbaum.

Luborsky, L., & McLellan, A. T. (1981). Optimal matching of patients with types of psychotherapy: What is known and some designs for knowing more. In E. Gottheil, A. T. McLellan, & K. Druley (Eds.), *Matching patient needs and treatment methods for alcohol and drug abuse* (pp. 51–71). Chicago: Charles C Thomas.

Luborsky, L., McLellan, A. T., Woody, G. E., O'Brien, C. P., & Auerbach, A. (1985). Therapist success and its determinants. *Archives of General Psychiatry, 42,* 602–611.

Luborsky, L., Mintz, J., Auerbach, A., Christoph, P., Bachrach, H., Todd, T., Johnson, M., Cohen, M., & O'Brien, C. P. (1980). Predicting the outcome of psychotherapy: Findings of the Penn Psychotherapy Project. *Archives of General Psychiatry, 37,* 471–481.

Luborsky, L., Rosenthal, R., Diguer, L., Andrusyna, T. P., Berman, J. S., Levitt, J. T., Seligman, D. A., & Krause, E. D. (2002). The Dodo bird verdict is alive and well—mostly. *Clinical Psychology: Science and Practice, 9,* 2–12.

Luborsky, L., Singer, B., Hartke, J., Diguer, L., Crits-Christoph, P., & Peterson, C. (1996). The context for sudden depressive mood shifts. In L. Luborsky (Ed.), *The Symptom-Context method: Symptoms as opportunities in psychotherapy* (pp.107–149). Washington, DC: American Psychological Association.

Luborsky, L., Singer, B., & Luborsky, L. (1975). Comparative studies of psychotherapies: Is it true that "Everybody has won and all must have prizes"? *Archives of General Psychiatry, 32,* 995–1008.

Luborsky, L., Stuart, J., Friedman, S., Diguer, L., Seligman, D. A., Bucci, W., Pulver, S., Krause, E. D., Ermold, J., Davison, W. T., Woody, G., & Mergenthaler, E. (2001). The Penn Psychoanalytic Treatment Collection: A set of complete and recorded psychoanalyses as a research resource. *Journal of the American Psychoanalytic Association, 49,* 217–234.

Luborsky, L., Woody, G. E., McLellan, A. T., O'Brien, C. P., & Rosenzweig, J. (1982). Can independent judges recognize different psychotherapies? An experience with manual-guided therapies. *Journal of Consulting and Clinical Psychology, 30,* 49–62.

Luhrman, T. M. (2000). *Of two minds: The growing disorder in American psychiatry.* New York: Knopf.

Main, M., Kaplan, N., & Cassidy, J. (1985). Security in infancy, childhood, and adulthood: A move to the level of representation. *Monographs of the Society for Research in Child Development, 50*(1–2), 66–104.

Malan, D. H. (1963). *A study of brief psychotherapy.* Oxford, UK: Charles C Thomas.

———. (1976). *The frontier of brief psychotherapy: An example of the convergence of research and clinical practice.* Oxford, UK: Plenum.

Mann, J. (1973). *Time-limited psychotherapy.* Cambridge, MA: Harvard University Press.

Marder, S. R. (2002). Evidence-based treatment for schizophrenia: A selected review. *Contemporary Psychiatry, 1,* 1–8.

Marmar, C. R., Weiss, D. S., & Gaston, L. (1989). Toward the validation of the California Therapeutic Alliance Rating System. *Psychological Assessment, 1,* 46–52.

Marziali, E. (1984). Three viewpoints on the therapeutic alliance: Similarities, differences, and associations with psychotherapy outcome. *Journal of Nervous and Mental Disease, 172,* 417–423.

McLellan, A. T., Luborsky, L., Woody, G., O'Brien, C., & Druley, K. (1983). Predicting response to alcohol and drug treatments: Role of psychiatric severity. *Archives of General Psychiatry, 40,* 620–625.

Menninger, K., & Holzman, P. (1973). *The theory of psychoanalytic techniques* (2nd ed.). New York: Basic.

Menninger, K. A. (1942). *Love against hate*. Oxford, UK: Harcourt Brace.

Menninger, K. A., Mayman, M., & Pruyser, P. W. (1962). *A manual for psychiatric case study* (2nd ed.). Oxford, UK: Grune & Stratton.

Miller, N., Luborsky, L., Barber, J. P., & Docherty, J. (Eds.). (1993). *Psychodynamic treatment research: A handbook for clinical practice*. New York: Basic.

Miller, S. J., & Binder, J. L. (2002). The effects of manual-based training on treatment fidelity and outcome: A review of the literature on adult individual psychotherapy. *Psychotherapy: Theory, Research, Practice, Training, 39* (2), 184–198.

Minuchin, S. (1974). *Families and family therapy.* Cambridge, MA: Harvard University Press.

Mitchell, J. (1995). Coherence of the relationship theme: An extension of Luborsky's core conflictual relationship theme method. *Psychoanalytic Psychology, 12,* 495–512.

Mitchell, S. (1999). Attachment theory and the psychoanalytic tradition: Reflections on human relationality. *Psychoanalytic Dialogues, 19,* 85–107.

Morgan, R., Luborsky, L., Crits-Christoph, P., Curtis, H., & Solomon, J. (1982). Predicting the outcomes of psychotherapy by the Penn helping alliance rating method. *Archives of General Psychiatry, 39,* 397–402.

Norcross, J. C, Hedges, M., & Castle, P. H. (2001). Psychologists conducting psychotherapy in 2001: A study of the Division 29 membership. *Psychotherapy: Theory, Research, Practice, Training, 39,* 97–102.

Norcross, J. C., & Hill, C. E. (2004). Empirically supported therapy relationships. *The Clinical Psychologist, 57,* 19–24.

Norcross, J. C., Karg, R., & Prochaska, J. O. (1997). Clinical psychologists and managed care: Some data from the Division 12 membership. *The Clinical Psychologist, 50*(1), 4–8.

Norcross, J. C., Prochaska, J. O., & Farber, J. A. (1993). Psychologists conducting psychotherapy: New findings and historical comparisons on the psychotherapy division membership. *Psychotherapy: Theory, Research, Practice, Training, 30,* 692–697.

O'Malley, S. S., Suh, C. S., & Strupp, H. H. (1983). The Vanderbilt Psychotherapy Process Scale: A report on the scale development and a process-outcome study. *Journal of Consulting and Clinical Psychology, 54,* 581–586.

Orlinsky, D. E., Grawe, K., & Parks, B. K. (1994). Process and outcome in psychotherapy: Noch einmal. In A. Bergin & S. Garfield (Eds.), *Handbook of psychotherapy and behavior change* (pp. 270–378). New York: Wiley.

Orne, M., & Wender, P. (1968). Anticipatory socialization for psychotherapy: Method and rationale. *American Journal of Psychiatry, 124,* 1202–1212.

Parloff, M. B. (1979). Can psychotherapy research guide the policy-maker? A little knowledge may be a dangerous thing. *American Psychologist, 34,* 296–306.

Pavlov, I. P. (1927). *Conditioned reflexes*. New York: Oxford Press.

Peralta-Ramírez, M. I., Jiménez-Alonso, J., Godoy-García, J. F., & Pérez-García, M. (2004). The effects of daily stress and stressful life events on the clinical symptomatology of patients with lupus erythematosus. *Psychosomatic Medicine, 66,* 788–794.

Perry, J. C. (1993). Defenses and their effects. In N. E. Miller, L. Luborsky, J. P. Barber, & J. P. Docherty (Eds.), *Psychodynamic treatment research: A handbook for clinical practice* (pp. 274–306). New York: Basic.

Perry, J. C., Luborsky, L., Silbershatz, G., & Popp, C. (1989). An examination of the methods of psychodynamic formulation based on the same videotaped interview. *Psychiatry, 52,* 302–323.

Pfeffer, A. Z. (1959). A procedure for evaluating the results of psychoanalysis: A preliminary report. *Journal of the American Psychoanalytic Association, 7,* 418–444.

Piper, W., Azim, H. F., Joyce, A. N., & McCallum, M. (1991). Transference interpretations, therapeutic alliance, and outcome in short-term individual psychotherapy. *Archives of General Psychiatry, 48,* 946–953.

Piper, W., Joyce, A. N., McCallum, M., & Azim, H. F. (1993). Concentration and correspondence of transference interpretations in short-term psychotherapy. *Journal of Consulting and Clinical Psychology, 61,* 586–595.

Ramzy, I. (1974). How the mind of the psychoanalyst works: An essay on psychoanalytic inference. *International Journal of Psychoanalysis, 55,* 543–550.

Ramzy, I., & Shevrin, H. (1976). The nature of the inference process: A critical review of the literature. *International Journal of Psychoanalysis, 57,* 151–159.

Rank, O. (1936). *Will therapy?* New York: Knopf.

Redl, F. (1966). *When we deal with children.* New York: Free Press.

Rogers, C. (1957). Training individuals to engage in the therapeutic process. In C. R. Struther (Ed.), *Psychology and mental health* (pp. 76–92). Washington, DC: American Psychological Association.

Rosenthal, R. (1990). How are we doing in soft psychology? *American Psychologist, 45,* 775–777.

Rosenthal, R., Blanck, P., & Vannicelli, M. (1984). Speaking to and about patients and predicting therapist's tone and voice. *Consulting and Clinical Psychology, 52,* 679–686.

Rounsaville, B., Glazer, W., Wilbur, C., Weissman, M., & Kleber, H. (1983). Short-term interpersonal psychotherapy in methadone-maintained opiate addicts. *Archives of General Psychiatry, 40,* 629–636.

Roy, C., Perry, J. C., Luborsky, L., & Bannon, E. (in press). Changes in defenses in completed psychoanalysis in the Penn Psychoanalytic Treatment Collection.

Safran, J. D., Crocker, P., McMain, S., & Murray, P. (1990). Therapeutic alliance rupture as a therapy event for empirical investigation. *Psychotherapy: Theory, Research, Practice, and Training, 27,* 154–165.

Safran, J. D., & Muran, J. C. (1996). The resolution of ruptures in the therapeutic alliance. *Journal of Consulting and Clinical Psychology, 64,* 447–458.

——. (2000a). *Negotiating the therapeutic alliance: A relational treatment guide.* New York: Guilford.

——. (2000b). Resolving therapeutic alliance ruptures: Diversity and integration. *Journal of Clinical Psychology, 56,* 233–243.

Safran, J. D., Muran, J. C., Samstag, L. W., & Stevens, C. (2001). Repairing alliance ruptures. *Psychotherapy: Theory, Research, Practice, Training, 38,* 406–412.

Safran, J. D., Muran, J. C., & Samstag, L. W. (1994). Resolving therapeutic alliance ruptures: A task analytic investigation. In A. O. Horvath & L. S. Greenberg (Eds.), *The working alliance: Theory, research, and practice*. (pp. 225–255) Oxford: Wiley.

Sampson, H. (1976). A critique of certain traditional concepts in the psychoanalytic theory of therapy. *Bulletin of the Menninger Clinic, 40,* 255–262.

Sandell, H. R., Blomberg, J., Lazar, A., Carlsson, J., Broberg, J., & Schubert, J. (2000). Varieties of long-term outcome among patients in psychoanalysis and long-term psychotherapy. A review of findings in the Stockholm Outcome of Psychoanalysis and Psychotherapy Project (STOPP). *International Journal of Psychoanalysis, 81,* 921–942.

Schachter, J., & Brauer, L. (2001). Post-termination patient analysis contact: Analysts' attitude and personal experience. *International Journal of Psychoanalysis, 82,* 1123–1132.

Schachter, J., & Luborsky, L. (1998). Who's afraid of psychoanalytic research? Analysts' attitudes towards reading clinical versus empirical research papers. *International Journal of Psychoanalysis, 79,* 965–969.

Schafer, R. (1991). Character, ego-syntonicity, and character change. In M. F. R. Kets de Vries & S. M. Perzow (Eds.), *Handbook of character studies: Psychoanalytic explorations* (pp. 169–189). Madison, CT: International Universities Press.

Schlesinger, H. (1969). Diagnosis and prescription for psychotherapy. *Bulletin of the Menninger Clinic, 33,* 269–278.

Schlesinger, H. (1977). The responsibility of the psychoanalyst for analytic and therapeutic change. *Bulletin of the Menninger Clinic, 41,* 202–206.

Seligman, M. E. P. (1995). The effectiveness of psychotherapy: The Consumer Reports study. *American Psychologist, 50,* 965–974.

———. (2002). Positive psychology, positive prevention, and positive therapy. In C. R. Snyder & S. J. Lopez (Eds.), *Handbook of positive psychology* (pp. 3–9). London: Oxford University Press.

Seligman, M. E. P., Castellon, C., Cacciola, J., Schulman, P., Luborsky, L., Ollove, M., & Downing, R. (1988). Explanatory style change during cognitive therapy for unipolar depressed patients. *Journal of Abnormal Psychology, 97,* 13–18.

Seligman, M. E. P., & Csikszentmihalyi, M. (2000). Positive psychology: An introduction. *American Psychologist, 55,* 5–14.

Selmi, P. M., Klein, M. H., Greist, J. H., & Sorrell, S. P. (1990). Computer-administered cognitive-behavioral therapy for depression. *American Journal of Psychiatry, 147,* 51–56.

Shabee, G., Blatt, S., Zaroff, D., & Pilkonis, P. (2003). Role of perfectionism and personality disorder features in responses to brief treatment for depression. *Journal of Consulting and Clinical Psychology, 71,* 629–633.

Shahar, G., Blatt, S. J., Zuroff, D. C., & Pilkonis, P. A. (2003). Role of perfectionism and personality disorder features in response to brief treatment for depression. *Journal of Consulting and Clinical Psychology, 71,* 629–633.

Shea, M. T., Elkin, I., Imber, S. D., & Sotsky, S. M. (1992). Course of depressive symptoms over follow-up: Findings from the National Institute of Mental Health Treatment of Depression Collaborative Research Program. *Archives of General Psychiatry, 49,* 782–787.

Shea, M. T., Elkin, I., & Sotsky, S. M. (1999). Patient characteristics associated with successful treatment: Outcome findings from the NIMH Treatment of Depression Collaborative Research Program. In D. S. Janowsky (Ed.), *Psychotherapy indications and outcomes* (pp. 71–90). New York: American Psychiatric Press.

Shevrin, H., Bond, J. A., Brakel, L. A. W., Hertel, R. K., & Williams, W. J. (1996). *Conscious and unconscious processes: Psychodynamic, cognitive, and neurophysiological convergences*. New York: Guilford.

Sifneos, P. W. (1972). *Short-term psychotherapy and emotional crisis.* Cambridge, MA: Harvard University Press.

Silberschatz, G. (1978). Effects of the analyst's neutrality on the patient's feelings and behavior in the psychoanalytic situation. *Dissertation Abstracts International, 39,* 3007.

Singer, B. A. & Luborsky, L. (1977). Countertransference: The status of clinical versus quantitative research. In A. Gurman & A. Razin (Eds.), *The therapist's handbook for effective psychotherapy*. (pp. 433–451) New York: Pergamon.

Siqueland, L., Crits-Christoph, P., Gallop, R., Gastfriend, D. R., Lis, J., Frank, A. Griffin, M. L., Blaine, J., & Luborsky, L. (2002). Who starts treatment: Engagement in the NIDA Collaborative Cocaine Treatment Study. *American Journal on Addictions, 11,* 10–23.

Sloane, R. B., Staples, F. R., Cristol, A. H., Yorkson, N. J., & Whipple, K. (1975). *Psychotherapy vs. behavior therapy.* Cambridge, MA: Harvard University Press.

Smith, M., Glass, G., & Miller, T. (1980). *The benefits of psychotherapy.* Baltimore: Johns Hopkins University Press.

Stern, D. (1985). *The interpersonal world of the infant*. New York: Basic.

Stone, L. (1951). Psychoanalysis and brief psychotherapy. *Psychoanalytic Quarterly, 20,* 215–236.

———. (1961). *The psychoanalytic situation.* New York: International Universities Press.

Strain, J. J., Newcorn, J., Wolf, D., & Fulop, G. (1994). Adjustment disorder. In R. E. Hales, S. C. Yudofsky, & J. A. Talbott (Eds.), *The American psychiatric press textbook of psychiatry* (2nd ed., pp. 671–680). Washington, DC: American Psychiatric Press.

Strupp, H. (1958). The performance of psychoanalytic and client-centered therapists in an initial interview. *Journal of Consulting Psychology, 22,* 265–274.

Strupp, H. H. & Binder, J. L. (1984). Psychotherapy in a new key: A guide to time-limited dynamic psychotherapy. New York: Basic.

Tang, T., & DeRubeis, R. (1999). Sudden gains and critical sessions in cognitive-behavioral therapy for depression. *Journal of Consulting and Clinical Psychology, 67,* 894–904.

Tang, T., Luborsky, L., & Andrusyna, T. (2002). Sudden gains in recovering from depression: Are they also found in psychotherapies other than cognitive-behavioral therapy? *Journal of Consulting and Clinical Psychology, 70,* 444–447.

Task Force on Psychological Intervention Guidelines. (1995). Template for developing guidelines: Interventions for mental disorders and psychosocial aspects of physical disorders. Washington, DC: American Psychological Association.

Thase, M. E., Greenhouse, J. B., Frank, E., Reynolds, C. F. III, Pilkonis, P. A., Hurley, K., Grochocinski, V., & Kupfer, D. J. (1997). Treatment of major depression with psychotherapy or psychotherapy-pharmacotherapy combinations. *Archives of General Psychiatry, 54,* 1009–1015.

Tichenor, V., & Hill, C. E. (1989). A comparison of six measures of working alliance. *Psychotherapy, 26,* 195–199.

Vaillant, G. (in press). Preface. *Mental health.*

Volpicelli, J. R., Pettinati, H. M., McLellan, A. T., & O'Brien, C. P. (2001). *Combining medications and psychosocial treatments for addictions: The BRENDA approach.* New York: Guilford.

Wachtel, P. (1993). *Therapeutic communication: Principles and effective practice.* New York: Guilford.

Wallerstein, R. (1986). *Forty-two lives in treatment.* New York: Guilford.

Wallerstein, R., & Robbins, L. (1956). The psychotherapy research project of the Menninger Foundation. Concepts. *Bulletin of the Menninger Clinic, 20,* 239–262.

Wallerstein, R., Robbins, L., Sargent, H., & Luborsky, L. (1956). The psychotherapy research project of the Menninger Foundation. Rationale, method and sample use. *Bulletin of the Menninger Clinic, 20,* 221–280.

Watson, J. B. (1913). Psychology as the behaviourist views it. *Psychological Review, 20,* 158–177.

Weiss, J. (1971). The emergence of new themes: A contribution to the psychoanalytic theory of therapy. *International Journal of Psychoanalysis, 52,* 459–467.

Weiss, J., & Sampson, H. (1986). *The psychotherapeutic process.* New York: Guilford.

Weissman, M. (1979). The psychological treatment of depression: Evidence for the efficacy of psychotherapy alone in comparison with, and in combination with pharmacotherapy. *Archives of General Psychiatry, 36,* 1261–1269.

Weston, D. (2002). Manualizing manual development. *Clinical Psychology: Science and Practice, 9,* 416–418.

Westen, D., Novotny, C. M., & Thompson-Brenner, H. (2004). The empirical status of empirically supported psychotherapies: Assumptions, findings, and reporting in controlled clinical trials. *Psychological Bulletin, 130,* 631–663.

Witkin, H., Lewis, H. B., & Weil, E. (1968). Affective reactions and patient-therapist interaction among more differentiated and less differentiated patients early in therapy. *Journal of Nervous and Mental Disease, 146,* 1930–2008.

Wolberg, L. R. (1967). *The technique of psychotherapy* (2nd ed.). New York: Grune & Stratton.

Wolitzky, D. L., Eagle, M., & Luborsky, L. (2001). Dynamic psychotherapy. In M. Hersen & V. B. Van Hasselt (Eds.), *Advanced abnormal psychology* (2nd ed. pp. 543–561). Dordrecht, Netherlands: Kluwer Academic Publishers.

Wolpe, J. (1969). *The practice of behavior therapy.* New York: Pergamon.

Woody, G., Luborsky, L., McLellan, A. T., O'Brien, C. P., Beck, A., Blame, J., Herman, L., & Hole, A. (1983). Psychotherapy for opiate addicts: Does it help? *Archives of General Psychiatry, 40,* 639–645.

Yalom, I. (2002). *The gift of therapy: An open letter to a new generation of therapists and their patients.* New York: HarperCollins.

Zander, B., Strack, M., Cierpka, M., Reich, G., & Staats, H. Assisted by J. Biskup, H. Homburg, S. Krannich, K. Ratzke, & I. Seide. (1995). Coder agreement using the German edition of Luborsky's CCRT method in videotaped or transcribed RAP interviews. *Psychotherapy Research, 5,* 231–236.

Zetzel, E. (1958). The therapeutic alliance in analysis of hysteria. In E. Zetzel (Ed.), *The capacity for emotional growth* (pp. 182–196). London: Hogarth.

Index

About the Authors

Lester Luborsky, PhD is professor emeritus of psychology in psychiatry at the University of Pennsylvania, where he has engaged in psychotherapy research for the past forty years. He is author of eight books and close to four hundred articles and chapters. He has received numerous professional awards including the Gold Medal Award for Lifetime Achievement in the Applications of Psychology from the American Psychological Association, and the Sigourney Award for Research in Psychoanalysis from American Psychoanalytic Association. He was recently honored by the Society for Psychotherapy Research with a celebration of his contributions to psychotherapy research.

Ellen Luborsky, PhD is a clinical psychologist in private practice, with training from the Cornell Medical Center and the New York University postdoctoral program in psychotherapy and psychoanalysis. She also consults and speaks on topics related to early development. She is coauthor, with Susan Klebanoff, of *Ups & Downs: How to Beat the Blues and Teen Depression.* She has also written articles on psychotherapy research and on play therapy. Her book *The View from the Sandbox* is forthcoming.

www.ingramcontent.com/pod-product-compliance
Ingram Content Group UK Ltd.
Pitfield, Milton Keynes, MK11 3LW, UK
UKHW012039150926
475560UK00001B/87

9 780765 704078